# Growing Up with Scoliosis
## (A Young Girl's Story)
### Written and Illustrated by Michelle Spray

Book Shelf, Inc.
PMB 111 • 1435 East Main St. • Torrington, CT 06790

Growing Up with Scoliosis
A Young Girl's Story
Written and Illustrated by Michelle Spray
© 2002, © 2009, 2011, ©2014, ©2015, ©2017

6th Edition: © 2017

ISBN-13: 978-1974579969
ISBN-10: 1974579964

Published by Book Shelf. Inc.
1435 East Main St., PMB 111
Torrington, CT 06790
www.havingscoliosis.com

All quotations and illustrations by Michelle Spray © 2002

Editor: Susan Pasternack
Medical Editor: Thomas S. Renshaw, M.D.
Photographer: Tracy Weed
Copyright © 2002, © 2009, © 2011, © 2014, ©2015, © 2017

# Follow Me on Social Media

I hope you enjoyed *Growing Up with Scoliosis*.
Please be sure to send me a review on www.amazon.com

To stay up-to-date on my next books
please subscribe to my e-mail list:
www.michellespraybooks.com/updates

**Follow me/like/share on social media:**
Facebook: www.facebook.com/MichelleSprayBooks
(for scoliosis) www.facebook.com/havingscoliosis

Twitter: www.twitter.com/SprayBooksEtc
(for scoliosis) www.twitter.com/michellespray3

Author website and blog: www.michellespray.com
(for scoliosis) www.havingscoliosis.com

Instagram: www.instagram.com/SprayBooksEtc

# Inspirational Quotes

Please visit my Etsy store for inspirational quotes:
https://www.etsy.com/shop/QuotesCreationsCT

# Why I Wrote This Book

Dear Reader,

I didn't even know what scoliosis was (let alone how to pronounce it) until I was diagnosed with it. Then I found out more than I ever wanted to know and thought that having scoliosis was the worst thing in the world to happen to me. Caught up in my own little pity party, I kept all my emotions inside: half the time my parents didn't even know what I was going through. (That's normal for a teenager, I guess.) Luckily, I kept a diary and that is how this book started. I would write down all my feelings without giving a second thought that anyone else in the world would ever read it, especially my family. At the time, I would have been mortified that my most private emotions would ever escape the peach pages of ink and marker, happiness and tears, that my diary kept secret. It was not until years later that I considered that sharing these thoughts and feelings might help others with scoliosis, or at least teach friends and family how to deal with it.

Please keep in mind that every case of scoliosis is unique: some never progress and new technology and procedures are being developed all the time, especially since I'd experienced them. Also remember that everyone copes differently. I can't say that I always took the best path, but I hope I can be a source of inspiration for others to learn from my experiences. Scoliosis is not the end of the world, even though it might seem like that to you right now. I can't even imagine not being here to share the story now, based on my thoughts and emotions then. This is why strong family support is crucial in a scoliosis patient's life.

So, with loving concern and utmost respect for scoliosis patients and their families, I hope this book helps you draw strength from each other when you need it the most.

Love,

Michelle

# Foreword

This is a very personal, individual, thoroughly comprehensive account of what the author felt and experienced while "Growing Up with Scoliosis." It begins with the school screening diagnosis and takes the reader through the stages of observation, long-term brace treatment, curve progression after the end of growth, and scoliosis surgery and its outcome.

The book presents things in a real-time, real-world frame of reference. It includes the emotional gamut of fears, anxieties, denials, acceptances, and more, and emphasizes the overriding perspective that one can grow and become a stronger person by successfully meeting and overcoming a challenge, especially a formidable one at a vulnerable time of life.

Although some of the technical aspects of the author's brace treatment and surgical care have evolved since she experienced them, the principles have not changed, nor have the scope and depth of feelings encountered by nearly every young person who must deal with scoliosis. The author has had the courage and concern for others to share her deeply personal experience. Countless young people will derive comfort and inspiration from her generosity.

Thomas S. Renshaw, M.D.

# Contents

# Contents

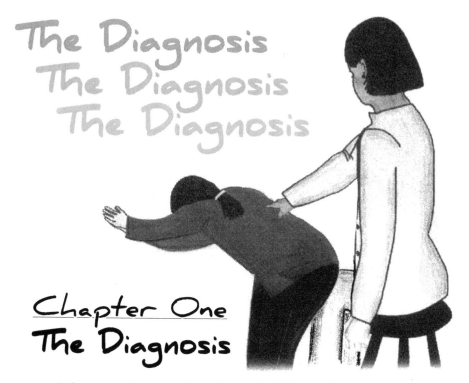

# The Diagnosis
# The Diagnosis
# The Diagnosis

## Chapter One
# The Diagnosis

It happened to me when I was in fifth grade. One day all the girls in my school had to bring their leotards to wear while they were being checked for a curvature of the spine called scoliosis (sko-lee-OH-sis). When it was time to get ready, we all piled into the lavatory and pushed each other out of the way so we could each get our own private stall where we would change. None of us knew what was happening so we waited for instructions. We changed clothes, threw our Catholic-school jumpers on over the leotards, and were then herded down the hallway to the nurse's office. When we arrived, we removed our jumpers and stood in our leotards waiting to be told what to do next.

One by one, we had to stand with our toes behind a white tape line that had been stuck to the cold, gray floor. We were told to bend over with our hands pressed together and our arms stretched out as if we were going to dive into a pool. The nurse ran her finger in a straight line down each of our backs to see if there was a curve. After all the girls were reviewed, we were sent to change once again and return to class—all except me. I had to sit and wait for all the other girls to finish before I could go.

"What is happening?" I thought to myself. "Why can't I go back? I don't have scoliosis."

After all the girls left, the nurse checked my back again. She wrote down something on a small white notepad, ripped off the first sheet, and told me to give it to my parents.

Infuriated, I thought, "What? She isn't going to tell me what it says. Is it serious? Am I going to die?"

Then I took a peek at the note. It said that I had scoliosis and that I should see a doctor. I still didn't understand.

"What's happening to me and what IS scoliosis?"

When I went home, I looked it up and read it aloud to myself: "Scoliosis is a curvature of the spine."

"What? I don't have that. I don't feel anything. The nurse is wrong. I feel fine."

The next thing I knew, I was sitting on a crisp, paper-covered table in the orthopaedic surgeon's office. I shivered as I sat there in my underwear and a backless paper shirt. I wasn't happy. Then, Dr. Perlman came in. He was very tall. My whole hand fit into his palm as he gave it a gentle squeeze hello. I looked up at him with my mouth open. We chatted for a few minutes and then I had to bend over again like I did in the nurse's office. He drew that familiar line down my back with his cold finger. I stood straight and bent over as much as I could to each side. Then I had to lie down and do leg stretches as instructed. I felt like it was all a waste of time.

"I don't have scoliosis, so what's taking so long?" I thought.

After checking my reflexes and neck movements, he traced my

spine again. Then I stood straight and he put his hands at my waist to see if my hips were even. He asked all the usual questions—did I have a "normal birth" and others like that. This was to rule out the possibility of any medical problems that might have caused the scoliosis. He also asked me how old I was and if I had had my first period yet. I thought I would just die of embarrassment. He explained that he needed this information so he could figure out when I would have my growth spurt. (It's during a growth spurt that a minor case of scoliosis can progress, or stay the same.) In girls, a growth spurt happens just after she develops breasts and gets her first period. In boys, it is just before he starts to grow facial hair. Thank goodness I didn't have to worry about any of that yet.

After the questions were answered, I walked down the hall to a small, cold room that smelled of chemicals. I held my paper shirt tightly so that it wouldn't open up as I walked. (It was bad enough that my doctor had seen my flowered cotton underwear. I didn't need everyone in the hallway getting a glimpse, too.) In the room there was a table, X-ray machines, and another little room with a tiny window in the door. I stood on the cold floor and something that looked like a tiny door with hinges pressed against my butt. The X-ray technician put a heavy, greenish-gray cloak-like thing around my shoulders and covered my chest to protect me from the radiation. It was a lead shield that reminded me of Superman's kryptonite.

The technician told me to breathe normally and stand still as she walked back to the little room with the tiny window on the door. Before she took the X-ray, she told me to hold my breath until she said OK. "All set," she said, and I thought we were done. But we weren't. The next thing I knew I had to walk over to the X-ray table to take some more X-rays while I lay flat and yet a few more while I was lying from side to side. Then we were done.

I quickly walked back to the examining room, where Mom was waiting. The paper-covered table was wrinkled with my butt imprint from when I had sat on it before. The paper crinkled as I hopped back up on the table, trying to prove that I was OK, that I didn't have anything wrong with me. Mom wanted to know how many X-rays were taken. After I told her, we just waited for the doctor to come in with the results. I looked around the room slowly. There wasn't much to see except the table I was on, some kind of white box on the wall, and a knee-knocker instrument on the counter. I was glad to find there were no needles.

Finally, my doctor came in carrying large black-and-gray plastic sheets, the X-rays. He shoved the top part of a sheet into the top part of the white box on the wall and the sheet stayed there, like magic. Then he flipped a switch and the box lit up and I was able to see my spine. He explained that scoliosis is any curve measuring over 10° and I had one measuring 17°. After hearing the news, I couldn't believe it. My mind reeled with questions but I was too shocked to ask anything.

"What does this mean? Is a 17° curve serious? Is it my fault? How can this be? Do I need to wear a body cast? Do I need to wear that neck thing? Will anyone notice? How can it be fixed? Will I still be able to dance? Will I need an operation? I don't feel anything," I thought to myself.

I looked at my mother and she seemed unusually calm, which actually had a similar effect on me. I thought, "Mom isn't flipping out, so it must not be a big deal." If she had freaked out, I probably would have, too.

My doctor assured me that at this point I didn't have to worry about anything at all because the curve was so slight.

What? Seventeen degrees didn't sound slight to me, but I took his word for it.

He gave me some exercises to do and suggested that I set up regular checkups to make sure the curve wasn't progressing. That sounded fine to me.

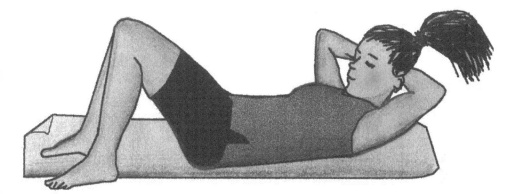

# Chapter Two
# The Curve Progresses

During the next year I went on regular checkups to make sure the scoliosis wasn't getting worse. The problem was that with each checkup, the X-rays showed that it was getting a little bit worse. Still, the curve was considered slight, in the 20° range, so I was told there wasn't anything to worry about. I felt fine. The only complaint I had was that somehow I was getting rough spots on my back from sitting in the hard chairs at school. Although the whole scoliosis thing didn't bother me that much, I could tell it bothered my parents. Each checkup meant hearing that the curve had progressed another degree, as minimal as it might seem. They felt like they were just sitting and watching because nothing could be done with a curve so slight. The good thing was that it still wasn't anything to worry about.

Between fifth and sixth grades, however, my back started to get really sore. I started to notice sharp, burning pains when my sister, Julie, and I were doing headstands in our room when we were supposed to be sleeping. I decided it might be a good idea to stop doing the headstands. My doctor gave me more exercises to do

11

in addition to the tap and jazz dance classes I was taking. The exercises wouldn't make the curve go away, but they would strengthen the muscles that held the spine in place and would keep me flexible. I tried to wrap my back in an Ace Bandage, but it didn't help. My doctor even tried to put a lift in one of my shoes to relieve the pressure on my back, but that didn't work either. I was scared that everyone would notice that something was wrong with me. I didn't want to look like a freak.

Since my sister and I shared a room, we used to stay up late giving each other back rubs. We fought over who would go second because the second person was able to get massaged to sleep, while the other one had to overcome the relaxed state and get to work. We spent hours fighting over how we wanted it done and whether one person got more minutes than the other. We often traded and compromised minutes of back rub for minutes of massage, or minutes of massage for minutes of back rub. Either way, someone always felt cheated because one of us would always be too tired and the "make it up tomorrow" never came. I think this is the reason I swore I would marry a masseur or resort to hiring one to give me back massages any time I needed. Actually, I think a masseur or a masseuse should be prescribed for all scoliosis patients.

By the time I got to seventh grade, my backaches were getting more and more persistent. I noticed the bump on my back was getting bigger and my siblings refused to give me back rubs. My doctor recognized that at this critical point in my growing years, the curve would not stop on its own. This time, the X-rays showed that my curve had progressed to a surprising 30° and something had to be done about it. Now.

I had to get a back brace. I wasn't happy. I couldn't believe it. All I kept thinking was that I had to wear a body cast that I couldn't take off and that would cover my entire body from my neck down. My doctor assured me that the brace would not be a full-body cast, that I could take it off, and that it would not be up to my neck. He told me a story about the very first brace, which had been made in Germany. It had a neckpiece with a tack under the chin so that if a patient slouched, he or she would get pricked. Uh! I felt better, after hearing the story, but I didn't want to wear a brace at all. It was the end of the world as I knew it.

My parents and I discussed this whole brace thing. I told them I wasn't getting one. But before I knew it, I had clothing that was a little bigger than I usually wore and I was walking into this tiny building to get my dreaded back brace. I wasn't happy.

The place looked like a dirty factory, only the dirt was white plaster and it was on the floor and tables. As I looked around, I saw flannel-clad workers putting together plastic pieces that looked like people's legs and knees and things. When a piece was finished, it was placed on the shelf along with other plastic body parts.

I was directed to a little room with a puke-yellow curtain missing a hook over the door. It might as well have not had a curtain on the door at all. To top it off, it was the skimpy kind of drapery that department stores have in dressing rooms. The kind that is an inch too short on both sides of the door, even if all the hooks happen to be there. I stood inside the dressing room and when I looked through the opening, I could actually see the front window of the building I was in and the people on the sidewalk outside. I was absolutely mortified.

I made my mother stand in front of one side of the door to block where the curtain didn't cover. I had to take off all my clothes and put on two body stockings, one over the other. Thank God there were two of these things, because just one was almost completely see-through. (Not that there was much to see, but when you're just starting to notice things and you're just getting used to a bra, you don't need anyone else to notice them also.)

When I was done putting the body stockings on, the cast maker came in. He shoved a long, thin piece of leather down the middle of my back, inside the body stocking, and along my spine. I had no idea why. I had to hold onto straps that were hanging from the ceiling; I felt like I was on the subway. My head was resting in some sort of holder to keep me standing straight and still, and a mold was made of my body the same way a cast is made. A roll of gauze was dipped in a pasty gray substance and it was wrapped around and around my body several times. It was warm, wet, and really gross. I had to wait in this contraption until the mushy gauze got hot, turned to plaster, and dried. I felt so stiff!

After the cast dried, it was cut off of me with something that looked like an electric pizza cutter. Now I realized why that piece of leather was put in there. I was so glad to get the cast off. I couldn't imagine what it would be like to have to wear it for longer than the time it took to make it. Once it was off, my body relaxed a little bit, but when I lowered my head, I was horrified to see that suddenly I was wearing only one wet, completely see-through body stocking. You could see everything. I went through all the swear words I could think of (to myself). It must have been cut off with the cast. I wanted to die. All that for a brace I didn't even want in the first place.

While Mom and I waited for the brace to be made, I saw all kinds of crutches, walkers, and more artificial body parts. It was weird. Then this white plastic "thing" with Velcro straps was handed to me. I wanted to take it and pass it on to the next person, but I knew it was for me.

Then, to my disappointment, I had to try the "thing" on. I didn't want to.

"Are they stupid? Of course it will fit. It's a mold of me!"

I was directed to a small dressing room, with a door this time. The door had horizontal slats and I could see everything in the

14

waiting room, but I was assured that no one could see me. I closed the door behind me and just sat on the tiny wooden bench, staring at the brace, wanting to cry.

I sat for a while until I was almost ready to put it on. My mother must have known I was stalling because she asked me if I was OK and if I needed help. I muttered a snippy, "No, I don't need help," through the slatted door. What I really wanted to say was, "Duh! How would you feel if you had to wear this thing? Just leave me alone."

The brace people gave me an undershirt to put on under the brace. I thought, "I'm finally old enough to wear a bra and now I can't?" They told me I couldn't wear one because it would be too uncomfortable.

"Yeah, OK, whatever."

I didn't realize what a project it would be to put the brace on. First, I flattened out the undershirt to make sure there were no creases or bunches. Then it was time to put the brace on. The plastic was so hard I could barely open the back of it to slip it on. Then, once I started to put it on, the undershirt got bunched up all over again. After a few attempts at keeping the undershirt wrinkle-free, I decided it didn't matter if the undershirt had a few creases in it.

"Who cares?" I thought. "No one is going to see it anyway. What's the big deal?" I just wanted to go home.

I guess I had the same "who cares" attitude about the Velcro straps. I couldn't get them tight enough. First, I couldn't reach them. It was like that itch on your back that you just can't get to. Once I found a strap, I had to thread it through a metal loop and pull as tightly as I could. Then, without letting go, I had to stick it onto the other side of the Velcro. For some reason, it kept getting loose again. Hot and impatient, I decided it was good enough. I got dressed and pulled my big underwear over the bottom of the brace, which covered my waist. I felt hideous. Once I was dressed, I

15

started walking toward my mother and I felt as if the brace was moving in one direction and my hips in the other. I knew it had to be tightened, but I just wanted to go home. I just wanted to be left alone.

Then...the car. Who thought it would be so challenging? I couldn't bend to get in. Then, once I finally flopped into the front seat, I couldn't bend to get out. Who thinks twice about bending to get in and out of a car?

When I got home, my siblings were outside waiting for me. When they saw me trying to get out of the car and thought I was in pain. I explained that nothing hurt; I couldn't move around all that well and it was just a matter of getting used to it. They seemed satisfied with that answer. Dad was waiting for me in the house. I was so happy when he asked me if I had it on. Couldn't he see it bulging out from underneath my clothes? Couldn't he tell I was walking so straight and tall? OK, well, I felt tall. You can't really look tall when you're 4'9, I suppose. Then I thought, "If Dad can't notice and he knows about it, maybe no one else will either. Maybe this won't be so bad after all."

I wasn't home for more than ten minutes when I already had an itch inside my brace that I couldn't scratch. I actually had been sent home with a pamphlet warning me not to stick pencils, rulers, or hangers down the brace to "relieve any itches." Sure! I couldn't wait until the few hours were up so I could take the brace off. I couldn't stand the smell of the plastic either. Dad said the smell would wear off in time. I hoped he was right.

scoliosis *scoliosis* *scoliosis*

# The Curve Progresses

Before long, I learned how to fasten the brace tightly, but comfortably. Yes, I did say the words brace and comfortably in the same sentence. It's weird how the tighter the brace was, the more comfortable it felt. I also learned how to breathe in shorter breaths and eat smaller meals more often during the day because the brace was so tight and restricting. Eventually, I got used to wearing it, even at night. Yes, I had to sleep in it, too. I had to wear this brace for twenty-three hours a day, and even though I hated it, I wore it faithfully. I had even given it a nickname. I called it my "T.C.," for torture chamber. I also lost my "who cares" attitude about the bunched-up undershirt. I found out what the big deal was all about. Let me explain it to you.

Think about the last time you wore a pair of socks that had elastic that was too tight. When you took them off, I'm sure you had a sock mark that you made worse by scratching. That is what it felt like to wear a skin-tight plastic brace over a crease in an undershirt. Only this mark was bigger, sweatier, and much more sensitive than that measly sock line. Trust me.

During my "hour of freedom," as I liked to call it, I did sit-ups, pelvic tilts, leg raises, arm stretches, waist bends, and other stretching exercises. It felt great after being cooped up in the stiff brace for so many hours. Then, I took a bath and rubbed alcohol on my back and hips to try to toughen up the skin. This would prevent rubbing sores, which formed when the brace wasn't tight enough. Then I washed the brace with soap and water. I could use any kind of soap except the green dishwashing kind because that made the padding inside the brace turn green. After this daily routine, I usually begged for a back massage from my family. I would say that "begged" is the right word to use because it usually took that much effort to finally get one. Dad was a good sport about it. He didn't mind, or at least he didn't show it. I would inch my way over to him and smile while he sat on the couch watching TV. How could he resist? After all, he knew a back rub was the greatest luxury in the world after I had been so stiff in my T.C. all day.

After Dad was done, I would sometimes see if Mom was willing to take up where he had left off. What a plan! Anyway, that was my day, every day, for a whole year—and that was the easy part about scoliosis and the brace.

# Chapter Three
# Growing Up with Scoliosis

The toughest part about growing up with scoliosis was not knowing how to handle it. I was in seventh grade and the kids didn't understand what I was going through. Some of them were really mean to me because they thought I had certain "privileges" that no one else had. They didn't understand why I was able to order my uniform gym shirt in a bigger size and wear it untucked while they couldn't. They didn't realize that sometimes when I ran, the gym pants would slide down my plastic waistline and lodge underneath the bottom part of the brace, making it impossible to pull them up without anyone noticing. It was much easier for me to have the pants slip down so long as the brace was still covered by my big shirt. Then, I could go into the bathroom and fix them later. I just didn't want anyone to know. I was so worried that someone would say something to me about it. I was in denial.

That was most of my problem. I took the wrong approach to dealing with my back brace from the very beginning. I became extremely sensitive and took everything to heart. Every piece of clothing I wore was my earnest and conscious effort to conceal my brace from anyone who didn't know I wore one. This was very difficult since I went to a parochial school. I ended up wearing my sweater for most of the year, even when it was hot. Instead of dealing with my back brace as if it were a knee or ankle brace, I felt like an awkward freak. As a result, I started to think that everyone else thought that, too, which probably wasn't the case at all. I didn't know how to react to myself in my new situation, so how could I expect anyone else to? At the time, though, I just felt that no one understood me. How could they? They didn't have to wear a brace. I felt bitter and wanted all of them to have to wear a back brace for a day to see how they would like it. I knew they wouldn't make it.

Let me give you some examples. No one realized what it took for me to learn how to tie my sneakers with the brace on. My breathing was restricted because the brace was working to keep me straight as I was trying to bend over, so I started sitting on the floor and resting one foot on the opposite thigh in order to tie that shoe. If I was in a hurry, I usually asked someone in my family to tie them for me. It got to the point where they wondered why I didn't just put my socks and shoes on before I put the brace on. I had no good reason except that it felt funny to put socks and shoes on before the rest of the outfit.

Even a simple thing like picking a pen up off the floor was a task, but I never let it stop me. If anything, it made me more determined to do it. If I was standing, I would bend my knees until I could touch the floor and the pen would be there, somewhere. I just had to feel for it. In school it became second nature—I could get out of my chair and bend down so quickly that no one in class even noticed. I would plan it. OK, no one's looking. Get ready, legs out from under the desk. Keep eyes on the object...GO! Then I would shoot out from behind my desk, pick up the pen or whatever I dropped, and get back in my chair, hoping no one saw the plastic hump on my back bulging out from under my sweater.

Speaking of embarrassment, one day I was sitting at my desk in class and dropped my pen, again. I decided this time that I would try to reach over and pick it up off the floor without getting out of my chair. I leaned over as much as I could. The bottom left side of my brace was pressing into the hard wooden chair, which made the top left part of the brace jam into my ribs. Still, I kept leaning over because I was so determined to reach the pen by myself and not ask any of my classmates, who didn't offer to help me anyway. Slowly and quietly I leaned and leaned until I thought I could reach it. I reached it all right! I landed on it! Yes, I fell right on the floor, in the middle of class. My butt got pinched between the hard plastic and the even harder cold floor. Everyone laughed and Sister Ellen ran over with her arms flailing. I think the embarrassment hurt more than the pinch. I returned to my chair, holding back the burning-hot tears.

---

That year, seventh grade, I became increasingly emotional, and a self-conscious wreck. I couldn't help but feel that I was *different*. I didn't feel that I fit in and that seemed like the most important thing to me. I was so insecure, but I didn't realize that we were all dealing with our own insecurities at the same time. Let's face it: seventh grade is hard enough when you don't have any reason for the kids to pick on you. Everything seemed so tragic, from pimples to talking to boys, or even deciding which deodorant to have your mom buy. Puberty was the onset of the ultimate self-consciousness for me and my back brace was an added nuisance.

As the days went on, I became more and more withdrawn. My self-esteem was disintegrating little by little and I started to question everything. I thought, "Why is this happening to me? Why did I get scoliosis? What did I do to deserve this? No boys are ever going to like me."

I kept asking questions like these a billion times a day. I wallowed in self-pity. Finally, I came to the conclusion that I might never know the answers. Even my doctor couldn't answer my questions. Scoliosis was just that unpredictable.

**?**

The year went on. I was in eighth grade and it was time to see Dr. Perlman for my regular checkup. This time the X-rays taken with my brace off showed that the scoliosis had progressed to 42°, a point at which Dr. Perlman could no longer treat me. I was devastated. I knew it could get to this, but never in a million years had I thought it would. It was time for me to see a scoliosis specialist at Newington Children's Hospital, about an hour from where we lived in Connecticut. Those were two words that absolutely horrified me—specialist and hospital. I didn't want to go. I went home and wrote in my diary.

I realized that the scoliosis was mine forever. It wasn't going to go away and that surprised me. For some reason I thought the brace would turn the curve back around. That was not what I was told, but that was what I wanted to hear. My curve was progressing, so instead of having a straight spine like this **(Figure 1)**, it was more like this **(Figure 2)**.

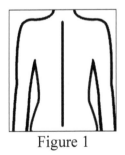

Figure 1

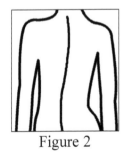

Figure 2

I looked bad in a bathing suit as well because instead of having a figure like this **(Figure 3)**, it was more like this **(Figure 4)**.

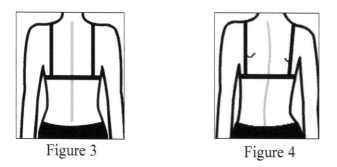

Figure 3                    Figure 4

My figure was curved really far in on one side and only a little bit on the other, which made me look as if I had no waistline on that side. It was clear that the next step was to see the scoliosis specialist. I was scared to death. I had never been to a hospital before. I had never even had a broken bone before. I hoped I didn't have to have an operation.

I ended up making the trip to Newington Children's Hospital. I went to school in the morning and left early so I would get credit for the day and still get my perfect attendance award at graduation. Once again I sat in the examining room on a paper-covered table. This time I was able to wear a cotton gown with ties in the back. It was much more comfortable than the paper gown at Dr. Perlman's and I felt like a person rather than just a patient.

The X-rays showed that the curve of my lower spine had gotten worse and a curve had started to form at the top as well. I couldn't believe it. How could it have gotten worse if I was wearing my brace as instructed for over a year? Fortunately, it was not bad enough to require surgery. They only operated on curves of 50° or more. Still, the fact was that I had to be put into a new and different kind of back brace. I was so scared it would be the kind that went up to my neck, which I thought would be the worst thing in the world to have to endure.

Dr. Renshaw, the scoliosis specialist, explained that it was normal for my spine to start to curve on top because it was just trying to straighten itself out. Also, my back wasn't just curving like this **(Figure 5)**, it was rotating this way, too **(Figure 6)**.

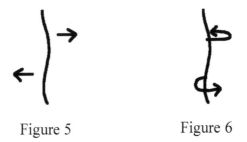

Figure 5               Figure 6

I was devastated. My doctor explained that the curve on top was a natural way for the spine to compensate for such a large curve on the bottom. This way the spine could keep the neck and head aligned with the rest of the body. Then, he explained how my spine had also started twisting. He gave me an example of a soup can. Imagine that the front of a can is how a normal spine looks. Well, my spine looked like a twisted can, where you could see some of the words from the front and some of the words from the back at the same time **(Figure 7)**.

Figure 7

My mother talked to Dr. Renshaw and the interns about getting the new brace. It wasn't even an option for me: I had to have it. Even though we were in the same room, all I was able to hear was a loud rumble of voices and an occasional phrase like "whether this one would help or not, because the other one didn't… blah, blah, blah." Suddenly a tear flew out of my right eye, then one from my left. Before I knew it, they were coming at the same time, too fast for me to soak up with my hand or push away from my face. I was embarrassed and bright red from crying in front of my doctor and three strangers with clipboards (interns from India). Once I started, I never looked up again until they had left. I couldn't wait to get out of there. Before we left, my mom made an appointment for me to get fitted for my new brace a few days later. It couldn't wait until school was out? I'd worked so hard for the perfect attendance award that now wouldn't be possible. I was not happy, to say the least.

ONE DAY
CAN CHANGE
YOUR LIFE
FOREVER
HOW IS UP TO YOU
Michelle Spray

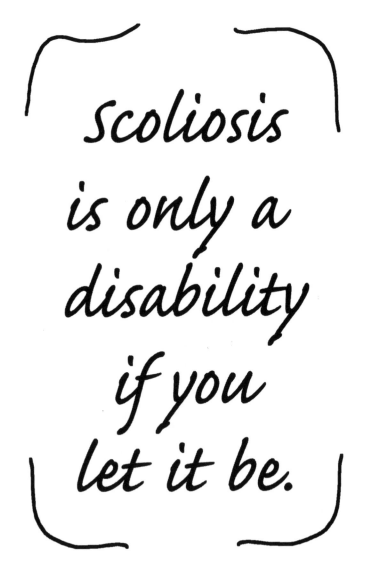

scoliosis
is only a
disability
if you
let it be.

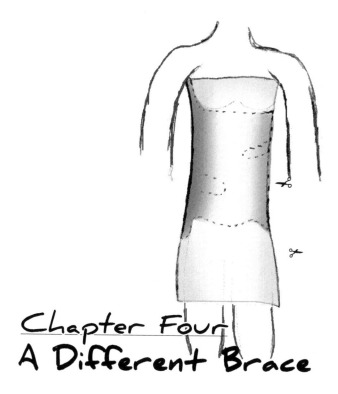

# Chapter Four
## A Different Brace

I got my new back brace in June of eighth grade and it was an all-day event. I went to the hospital in the morning and they gave me a room to check into, and a roommate. She couldn't wait to get her new brace so she could stand up straighter. I couldn't believe it. I couldn't believe this was happening to me while she was happy?

It was time to get fitted for our braces. This was a very different experience from when I got my first one. This time, besides the fact that I had a friend, I didn't have to get a mold made of my body. Instead, I had to put something on that looked like a really big tube of white plastic. I had to pry it open like the other brace, but this one was much tougher to open and the plastic and glue smelled really strong. It covered my whole body—from my armpits over my butt, to my thighs. Once I had it on, an intern drew pencil marks on the plastic to determine where to put certain thick and thin pieces of padding inside the brace. Then, he drew marks to determine where my hips were, where my breasts should be, where my butt ended, and where the airholes should go. He had a nervous giggle, which started to annoy me. I was the one who should have been nervous.

When he was done, I took off the tube and it was cut down to size.

After it was cut, I saw it and thought I would just die.

"No, that can't be it. It's so big. No!"

Reluctantly, I put it back on and the intern drew a few more pencil marks on the plastic before I took it off to get it cut down a little more. I hoped it would be cut down a lot more. After all the adjustments of placing the padding and sizing and more cutting, the brace was finished. I was disappointed in how big it still seemed. I didn't know how I was supposed to walk around in the thing. No wonder they called it the "Boston brace." I felt like I was the size of Boston when I wore it.

It was so different from my other one **(Figure 8)**. Instead of a small, girdle-like, solid, heavy piece of plastic with thick Velcro straps in the back, this one was bigger and had more airholes, but the plastic was thinner and more lightweight. From the front **(Figure 9)** it was high under the left arm, had airholes, was long over the left hip, and ended one-quarter inch from the chair, if I was sitting down. From the back **(Figure 10)** there was a large airhole on the side, buckles, Velcro straps, glued-on reinforcement pieces, and tiny airholes in various spots. I had to wear my big underwear pulled over the brace, again.

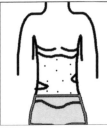
Figure 8

Figure 9

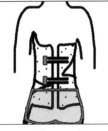
Figure 10

# A Different Brace

After I wore the brace for a while, there was a really tender spot on my back from where it was pushing. It felt as if I had an exposed nerve or something. The doctors weren't sure what was causing that one spot to get swollen and tender and they wanted me to go for a bone scan to see what it might be. They didn't find anything.

My roommate for the day didn't have any problems with her brace at all. I was sent for a few more adjustments, but it didn't feel any better. The pain was unbearable, yet I was sent home "to get used to it." What was to get used to? I already spent a whole year in a back brace; I knew it wasn't supposed to hurt.

I was put on a schedule to work up to twenty-three hours a day of brace wear. The sensitive spot was really painful and it never let up, even for a minute, no matter how I stood or sat or lay down. Finally, after two weeks and many complaints, bad moods, and miserable feelings, I went back to the hospital. The reinforcement piece of plastic was taken off the left side of the brace. What a relief! You know the feeling you have when your headache finally goes away? That's how I felt. I was so happy. I felt great, like a new person. I was actually able to survive the new "torture chamber."

Even though the brace felt much better, it was still more restricting than the other one, but this was a good thing. For the first time in more than a year, my spine was kept securely in place and my back felt great. This brace brought my curve within the brace down to 31° and I didn't have to go back for a checkup for two months. I was happy until I realized I had wear the thing to school.

Luckily, I only had a couple weeks until graduation. In the meantime, I had to wear the new brace for a few hours a day, then eventually, the dreaded day came when I had to wear it to school and keep it on all day. I was so nervous. I didn't know what to expect. It was the end of the school year so it was really hot. I was sweaty, uncomfortable, and extremely self-conscious that everyone would see the brace bulging from underneath my shirt and ask me about it. I wondered if anyone could smell the plastic and glue.

It made me want to gag the first few times I wore it. But the smell wore off eventually and I was able to finish the last few weeks of elementary school.

I couldn't wait to graduate. My parents assured me that high school would be different; I knew it would be. It had to be. I had been with the same kids since kindergarten. We all moved up together, grade by grade, year after year, progressing down the hall one more room until eighth grade. We never had the opportunity to switch rooms, ever. The teachers came to us, except for gym and recess, so we sat in the same seats all year long. The routine got tiring. I couldn't wait to see some new faces and new surroundings.

---

I was also looking forward to summer vacation and some new sights. We went to Rhode Island, to see the Tall Ships. We walked, yes, walked, everywhere, miles around Newport, from mansion to mansion. I got sores from rubbing against the brace in the hot weather. I was very uncomfortable.

That summer I also got my first pair of contact lenses, which I knew would help my self-esteem in high school. I hoped that things would be different for me, that I would make some friends at last. And I was hoping that among those new people in my life would be a boyfriend.

# Chapter Five
## Getting Adjusted

After a few weeks of wearing my new brace and getting used to it physically, I realized that no one was aware I had it on unless they knew me. Sometimes, even people who knew I wore a back brace asked me if I had it on and that made me feel good. I thought that everyone who saw me knew. It was a good thing that big clothes came in style that year because I was able to hide it well. But when someone bumped into me, that was a different story. One time, a guy accidentally jammed his finger into my brace at a store and demanded to know what was "under there." I just stared at him and didn't answer. Why did he have to know anything? After that I got brave and told people I had a back brace on and they would get quiet and concerned because they would think I had been in some sort of serious accident.

It was only a matter of time before the hotter weather came. Then, even worse, was the sweltering weather. I thought the new brace would be better than the old one because it had bigger airholes in it. But the heat felt the same. I learned how to put cornstarch on my skin before I put on the long, seamless cotton undershirt and strapped myself into my new "T.C." The powder helped soak up most of the moisture but sometimes I still got prickly heat. My whole stomach and back knew what it felt like to be a baby's bottom.

My undershirt was sopping wet under the brace. Worse than that was changing the undershirt and putting the brace right back on again while the padding was still damp. Procrastination was not an option. The quicker I got it back on, the less I had to think about it, and the sooner I got over the initial gross feeling. Someone should design a more breathable brace with interchangeable padding inside. Of course, I should get paid the royalties for inventing it. Anyway, sometimes I found that it was better to have the wet undershirt stick to me and peel it off later than to tease me with a clean, dry undershirt and a damp brace on top of that. It was much better to take the brace off for my allotted hour and let it dry. Then I had an hour to work up enough nerve to put it back on again.

One good thing about the summer was that I could remove the brace to go swimming. The water actually created pressure on my body that acted like a brace. That summer my dad nicknamed me "Fish." The only thing was that I didn't want anyone to see what I looked like in a bathing suit. Once I finally got the nerve to go in the water, it usually took a lot more nerve to come out. So while I had no waistline on the left side and a very exaggerated waistline on the right, I also had a bump in the lower left section of my back **(Figure 11)**. There was nothing I could do about it except to wear T-shirts over my bathsuit in the water.

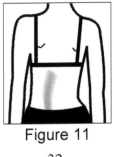

Figure 11

I also wore T-shirts over my leotards at dancing school. Yes, I wore my brace to dancing school. Although I couldn't move around all that well, I never let the brace stop me. Except maybe when it came to boys.

I thought that if a boy found out that I had scoliosis, he wouldn't like me. I was afraid to go to school dances because I didn't want a boy to feel the brace. I was equally scared to go to the dances without the brace on because I didn't want a boy to feel my uneven waistline or the bump on my back and ask me what it was. There was just something scarey about telling someone that your spine is protruding from the skin on your back. Anyway, not wearing my brace was never anything more than a fantasy.

My next checkup was in August and my curve inside the brace had progressed to 37°, but no one seemed to be too concerned. I was wearing the brace and doing the exercises and that was all anyone could do. Actually, I enjoyed doing the exercises because they made me feel better after being so stiff all day. I couldn't wait to start high school, where I wanted to join the swim team for extra strengthening. My doctor was thrilled to write me a note and thought it was a great idea. To my disappointment though, I was slow. I couldn't catch my breath. I wasn't good and I didn't end up making the team. But everything happens for a reason, right?

"I realized that no one knew
I had it on unless they knew me."

Whisper

Whisper

whisper

## Chapter Six
# Braced for School

Scoliosis had had a major impact on my life in grammar school, frustrating me both mentally and physically. I was very self-conscious about my body, constantly worrying about what other people thought or what they were saying about me. I always assumed the worst, and you know what they say about the word assume—ass-u-me, it makes an a$$ out of you and me. Maybe I assumed wrong. Who knows? They might not have been talking about me at all. Unfortunately, I didn't realize this until I started high school.

One of my first positive experiences in high school was with a great guy named Michael. He used to try to tickle me through the big airholes on each side of the brace. Sometimes he would aim too high or too low and catch his finger on the hard plastic, saying he would get me the next time. Sometimes he would aim just right. His friendship caught me off guard and for the first time I actually felt like a real person. It gave me hope that others might see me that way, too. He was able to look past my plastic body to what was inside and that made me happy. Too bad he had a girlfriend.

Of course, there had to be some immature kids who were not as understanding. I remember a hefty blond kid and his dark-haired friend. One day they saw me bending over to get something out of my locker. The brace was bulging from underneath my sweater and I heard them say something about the Hunchback of Notre Dame. I just looked at them and then away before my eyes filled up with those burning-hot tears I knew so well. Their laughter seemed to echo through the hallway. And I had hoped high school would be completely different.

Michael helped me brush it off and I didn't let it bother me after that. My good experiences far outweighed the bad. I had to keep that in mind as I went through this journey I had friends who accepted me, my brace, and my back as a package deal. They tried to understand the best they could, but it was hard for them to put themselves in my place.

There were many small experiences, some amusing, some not, that took place during this time. On one occasion I went to hang my purse on the back of my chair, but it got caught on the back of the brace instead. I didn't even notice at first, so I went through class with a bag hanging from my back. I hoped no one else had noticed.

I wore the brace to gym class, where I ran around and played basketball and floor hockey. I was able to run fine, and if anyone bumped into me, they were the ones who got hurt, not me. Sometimes the brace was a definite advantage.

# Braced for School

By December of my freshman year in high school my scoliosis had progressed to 40°. I agreed to remain faithful to my exercises although by that time I was convinced they were not doing much good. I wore the brace all school year and even wore it during a ten-mile walk-a-thon. I thought I could do it. Unfortunately, the brace rubbed on my hips and made them red and raw. But it was worth it. I spent the day walking and laughing with my friends. They were the ones complaining that their feet hurt, while I just kept going. There was no stopping me from finishing with everyone else. We even passed by my street, but I didn't go home. It was one of my many accomplishments in my new T.C.

In May of that year I performed in my first high school musical. I danced around on stage with my brace hidden under the costumes. No one noticed and I had a blast. At my checkup that month, my curve measured 41°. When would it stop?

In September, at the beginning of my sophomore year in high school, I went back for yet another checkup. I hated to go; each time my curve got a little bit worse and there was nothing anyone could do about it. It seemed to be so automatic: every few months I went in and every few months I was told a higher number and sent home. No big deal, not anymore. But this time I knew I was having problems. My brace didn't fit that well. My body was curved too much and I had more skin irritation than usual. Also, I had started to get twinges of pain in my ribs on the left side. Actually, I wasn't really sure if it was my ribs. I just knew the pain was there, near my ribs, under my left breast.

At that checkup the curve inside the brace measured 42°. Just hearing the number climbing ever so slowly was torture enough. Why couldn't it just stop? I was doing everything right. So maybe that was why I swore I could hear things rubbing every time I breathed. Everyone thought I had imagined it. I even opened my mouth as wide as I could to make people listen while I inhaled, but no one heard it. (Sometimes I would even get sharp pains from taking very deep breaths.)

After a while the pain in my back became a sharp, constant, pain that bothered me whenever I stood for a short period of time, sat for a while, or even walked around. It hurt no matter what I did. But I didn't let it stop me. I never stayed home from school because of it. I never missed homework or went to bed without studying because of it. It would have been so easy to use scoliosis as an excuse, but I never did. When I felt a little down, I wrote my feelings in my diary and then always found something else to keep me busy. Moping about it was something I had tried before and it never helped.

Four months later, in January of my sophomore year of high school, I was allowed to keep my brace off for a whole day before my next X-ray. I was thrilled. I went to school smiling and people recognized that there was something different about me. I tried to stand and sit up as straight as possible. As the day went on, though, I felt terrible. My body was crooked and my skirt was as well. My back was really sore and I didn't think I would make it through the day without being slumped over because it hurt so much. I quickly realized that I depended too much on my dreaded brace to keep me standing and sitting straight. I never thought I would hear myself say I couldn't wait to put my brace back on.

The next day I had a series of X-rays taken without my brace which showed that my curve had progressed to a whopping 54°. Again, I couldn't believe what I was hearing. Each checkup was another disappointment; I couldn't take it anymore. I wondered why this was happening to me. This time I also had X-rays taken of my wrists, a method doctors rely on to check a patient's bone age rather than chronological age. With this information they could calculate when I would stop growing and how long they would have to watch the progression of my curve. They determined that I had had my growth spurt within the last year and a half and that I would not be growing anymore. Hurray for me to know that I would stand at the gigantic stature of 4'10" for the rest of my life!

The result of the wrist X-ray showed that I had already reached skeletal maturity; the brace would no longer work to correct the curvature of my spine. What? Yes. The words felt like a knife stabbing me in the heart over and over again.

"That's it?" I thought. "I have a crooked spine. I was experimented on for months and years with back braces and I'm done growing and that's it?" I couldn't bear to go without my brace for a whole day. I felt like a wrung-out mop, trapped inside a mangled body, and that's it? Good-bye?

I thought there should have been more to it, like I was missing something. It was as if I had worn the brace for so long hoping for a different outcome and when I heard it, I still waited for something else, something closer to what I had hoped. I felt like a little kid going trick or treating and seeing a full bowl of candy and being handed only a tiny box of raisins. I just stood there—confused, hurt and cheated.

I was advised to wean out of the brace gradually over a period of two weeks and continue my exercises. I knew this was necessary, especially since my back was so sore after being unbraced for only twenty-four hours. Finally, after all that time, I was brace-free. But what was next?

? ? ? ? ? ? ?

**"** I couldn't bear
to go
without my brace
for a whole day.
I felt like a
wrung-out mop... **"**

# Chapter Seven
# What's Next?

Dr. Renshaw presented the options to me: I didn't want to hear any of it. All I did was wallow in the fact that I had worn two back braces over a period of three long, hot summers and they hadn't done any good. He explained that if I had never worn a brace at all, I would have been crippled. I was shocked by his answer. I tried to understand. The brace slowed the progression of my scoliosis quite a bit. The only thing to do now was to watch the curve and discuss the options at the next visit. If my curve progressed significantly within the next four months, then a "posterior spinal fusion with Cotrell Dubosset instrumentation to preserve motion segments and saggital plane contouring" would be recommended.

"If the curve remains in the low 50° range," he explained, "then it is borderline and we will discuss the pros and cons of continued observation versus surgical correction." Even with all the big words, I understood what it meant. I started to cry. There was no way I was having an operation and that was that. It was the end of the story as far as I was concerned.

Before I left his office, I decided to mention that I thought I could hear something rubbing against my lungs whenever I moved or twisted. He said I was right and if the curve worsened and I didn't have the operation to correct it, there was the possibility that my curving spine and/or reshaping ribs could actually puncture my lungs. Still, I thought, I was not having an operation.

— — —

I continued my sophomore year in high school, keeping busy with every extracurricular activity I could find and having a great time. I was so happy being busy. I tried out for the spring musical and I actually brought sheet music with me so I could audition for a lead. My mother thought I was being silly because she didn't think I could sing; no one did. I never sang around the house. I certainly surprised her when I came home with the part of Amaryllis in *The Music Man*. It was so much fun! Despite the constant pain, I sang and danced around the stage. Before I knew it, I was standing near a piano, doing vocal exercises with my new voice coach.

In May I went back to the hospital: my curve measured 53°, plus I had grown a quarter of an inch. I didn't think I was supposed to grow anymore. Six months later, in November of my junior year of high school, my curve had progressed to 56°. In my heart I knew what had to be done; I just didn't want to do it. So with each check- up, we put off the inevitable with another six months to think about it.

Soon it was May again. My junior year had flown by. I was still in dancing school and continuing my other extra activities, including a role as a Havana dancer in my high school production of *Guys and Dolls*. This was great for me physically because we practiced after school and it helped keep my back in shape. But even though I kept myself very busy, subconsciously, I was counting the days.

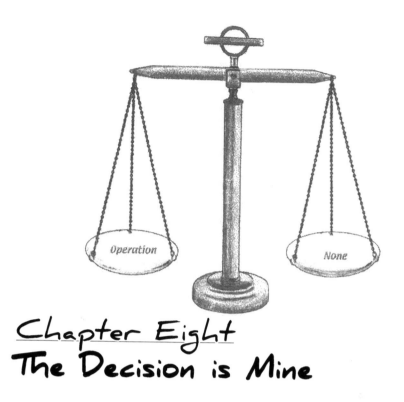

# Chapter Eight
## The Decision is Mine

The time was upon me and as much as I didn't want to think about what was happening, I had to. It was unavoidable. I weighed out and brainstormed all the possibilities in one, big, steady stream of consciousness.

"How many sixteen-year-olds have to make a decision like this," I asked myself. "What do I want: The bump on my back or the scar? The constant pain of scoliosis or the temporary pain of recovery? Will I be able to go to my senior prom? Will I be able to make the senior class trip? Will I be able to perform in my last high school musical? I will be going to college the year after. When will I have time to do it? I don't want to take time off between high school and college. I want to start college on time. During college? After college? I'll have a career. I won't be able to take time off. What about kids? I won't be able to do it then. I won't have time. The pain or the scar? A bump or none? When should I have this done? Do I want to have this done? I'll have a flat back and a nice figure. I want that. I really want that. What should I do? I want the pain to go away. I have to have the operation. I have to find the time. I have to have it done now. I want to have it done as soon as possible. I want to have a flat back for next summer. Yes, I'm going to do it!"

## " I'm going to do it!"

As soon as I made up my mind to have the operation, I knew it was the right decision. There was no going back and I never second-guessed myself. I felt in control of my own body at last. The scoliosis had taken over my whole body; finally I felt that I wasn't going to allow it to cripple me and keep me self-conscious until the day I died. I deserved to have a great-looking body and this was how I would have it. I was ready.

I waited a few days to tell my parents my decision and that gave me time to think in private. They were sitting on the couch when I marched down the stairs, stood in front of them, and just blurted out that I was going to have the operation. They asked if I had really thought about it; they wanted to be sure I was making the right decision. There was no doubt in my mind that I had.

I think my parents were in some way ready for what I told them because they said I had seemed snippy and in deep thought for a few days. When it came down to it, I just couldn't handle the pain any longer. I just wanted to be fixed already.

When I returned to the doctor in May, my scoliosis had progressed to a "left thoracolumbar curve of 57° with one centimeter decompensation in the spine." Once again Dr. Renshaw discussed the options with us. He said it was likely that without surgery I would have "continued progression, continued decompensation, and continued back pain," which I was already having on a daily basis, particularly after sitting in school. Then we discussed the risks of having this operation—"death, paralysis, infection, failure of fusion, instrumentation failure, transfusion-transmitted disease, and all other potential complications." We also discussed my age. I could have it done now or later, when there would be other factors and risks involved.

About the only thing I wanted to know was how much it would hurt. No one could give me a straight answer. It didn't matter anyway; my decision had already been made. I literally couldn't stand living that way anymore. Through crying eyes I told my doctor I was going through with it; there was no going back. I decided that if I couldn't have it done that summer, I wanted to wait to finish my senior year without interruption and have it done after graduation. We set the date for two months later, July 20. After that, everything just seemed to follow.

10   months   9   8   7   4

11   weeks   5

6   3

2   **DAYS**

# Chapter Nine
# Counting the Days

1

To prepare for my operation, my mother started looking for books about scoliosis; there wasn't much to read except a few medical volumes. That was frustrating, so Mom got the phone number of a girl from Newington Children's Hospital who just had the same procedure. Her mother was having a fit because her daughter had gone on an upside-down ride at a nearby carnival just a few months after her operation; it hadn't affected her at all.

"If she could do it, so can I," I thought.

Our mothers wanted the two of us to talk, but I didn't want any part of it. I didn't want to talk about it; I didn't want to know about it; I didn't want to know the details about the operation in any way—not the process, not the recovery, nothing. I was having this operation and that was all I needed to know, and more than anyone else had to know. I didn't want anyone to find out. I didn't want sympathy; I just wanted to get it over with.

In no time at all, my mother's friends were asking me about my back and whether I needed their blood. Was that supposed to make me feel better? I couldn't believe how many people knew. I thought I would just die from embarrassment

Everyone thought I was acting pretty silly about the whole situation. They asked me if I really thought I could hide such a major thing like a spinal fusion. Yeah. Yeah, I did. Why should everyone know? I felt that it was one of the few things I had that should have been kept private, but it wasn't. I found that keeping a diary helped me to vent a lot of the frustration I was feeling.

I wrote: "June 1—If one more person asks me how my back is I think I might just burst out crying in their face. Everyone knows. Somebody might as well put it in sky writing, or, even better, on a billboard on my front lawn. Please! I just want to enjoy the rest of the summer without thinking about my scoliosis. Even all the babysitting jobs are going to my sister because they think I can't lift the kids. Why? I feel the same now as I did months ago, even a year ago. Everyone is so dumb."

━ ━ ━ ━ ━ ━ ━ ━ ━ ━ ━ ━

That June was our junior prom. I wore a dress that was a little bit big so it would fit loosely around my waist and hide the bump. My date and I danced almost the whole night through. We changed at my house afterward to go to an after-party and he told my mother that his "feet hurt from dancing so much!" I thought it was a great compliment to me.

After that I just seemed to be counting down the days until my operation. Naturally, I was on edge and my family took the brunt of my frustration. We found that sometimes we got along better when I didn't speak to them. I just wanted to enjoy as much summer as possible, but everything seemed to be a reminder, a very stressful reminder. I had about a month and a week to go.

School was almost over, but not quite. Living in New England, we had to make up the snow days we missed from the winter, so they were tacked onto the end of the year. These days were called "busy days" and completely pointless since all the grades were closed. It was babysitting in my opinion.

The classrooms were sweltering and my back was killing me. I just wanted to go home. Finally, we were called to the gym for an assembly to discuss stress. Great! Just what I wanted to hear, someone talk about stress. "Nobody here knows what stress is," I thought to myself.

On the way out of the classroom, a teacher stopped me and asked how I was feeling. I thought to myself, "Oh no, be careful. Don't scream at the top of your lungs or barrel over the top of the desk and knock her out." I zoned back in. She had "heard" that I was going to have "surgery" and asked me when "the big day" was. She said it so matter-of-factly and loudly in front of everyone. It was like I was going to celebrate or something. I almost cried on the spot. I was so scared and no one was willing to let me forget.

# STRESS

**S**pine

**C**urvature

**O**rthopaedist

**L**ateral curve

**I**mage

**O**bstacles

**S**elf-esteem

**I**diopathic

**S**chool screening

e
x
e
r
c
i
s
e

vitamins

nutrients

vegetables

iron

fruit

water

## Chapter Ten
# Preparations

A month before the operation, I went to the local branch of the American Red Cross to donate my blood for the transfusions I would need. I didn't want to worry about getting a disease from getting someone else's blood, so I donated my own. When I got there, my blood pressure was taken, and the tip of my finger was pricked to test my blood. Because I was underage and underweight, I wasn't allowed to give blood for the blood bank. You need to be at least eighteen years old and over one hundred pounds, regardless of your health. Luckily, however, I was able to give blood for myself.

The first time I went to donate the nurses couldn't get any blood out of me and it took such a long time, which was unusual. They said it was because my veins were too small, but I knew it was because I wasn't drinking enough liquids. I was supposed to drink tons of fruit and vegetable juices and eat lots of vegetables that were high in vitamins so that when I got the blood back through the transfusion, I would regain the vitamins I had lost during the operation. I learned my lesson. From then on, I drank juice every time I thought of it. I also had to take iron pills, which did terrible things to my stomach. I gained weight from water retention but at least I didn't have any more problems giving blood.

Every time I went back to the Red Cross my finger was pricked to check my cell count. Then a drop of my blood was put on glass slides for inspection under the microscope. Next I got a slip of yellow paper with all my technical information for the day, including my weight, blood pressure, etc. Then it was time to sit in the big yellow chair. I knew the routine.

The big chair was the cushiony, vinyl kind, like a dentist's chair, where you can put your feet up. I wondered why it had to be yellow. I hopped up, lay back, and the nurse applied disinfectant on my arm by the elbow crease. Then she tied a piece of elastic really tightly around my arm to cut off the flow of blood. I didn't watch the rest; I closed my eyes and felt a prick. I had to keep squeezing and releasing a tiny ball in my hand while I waited. By accident I opened my eyes and saw the man next to me giving blood. I actually saw the blood running through the plastic tubes and filling up the plastic bag on the floor; it was dark purple.

After my blood was taken, a piece of cotton was placed on the spot where the needle had been and held in place by a brown cloth Band-Aid. Then I had to wait in the chair and keep my arm elevated until the nurses said I could go. They wanted to make sure I didn't faint from loss of blood; I thought that was silly. While I was waiting, I saw other people who said they felt faint or dizzy and they seemed to be overplaying the whole deal. I thought, "Give me a break. Don't be wimps."

After a few minutes the nurse said I could get up. I felt a little weak, but I didn't want to say anything. The nurse walked me over to the kitchen where there were other people who had just given their blood having a feast of cookies, granola bars, crackers, and juice. They started bragging about how much blood they'd given to the blood bank so far. I wondered whether I would be able to handle having my blood taken on a regular basis like that.

# Preparations

While I was in the kitchen, I was served my choice of snacks and more juice. I thought I would just float away. I couldn't stand drinking all the fruit and vegetable juices, especially when I wasn't thirsty. When I was done, I got up and almost passed out. I sat back down quickly and decided not to make fun of the wimpy people anymore. Eventually, after a few more visits, my blood collection was complete and it was frozen until my July 20th date with my surgeon.

---

Soon school was out and I tried to enjoy summer vacation. The only thing I had to give up for a while was the sun. The last thing I needed was to recover from my operation and sunburn at the same time. Instead of enjoying the beach, I went to the mall, sketched in my art pad, or wrote in my diary. Unfortunately, these quiet moments gave me more time to think about what lay ahead. I couldn't believe that I had made such a major decision on my own. I was very proud.

Although I couldn't wait to feel better, I wished that there was a simpler answer. Then I discovered one: a miracle pill that twists the spine back over time the same way that it curled into this hideous shape over the years. If the spine can become like an angry snake and move around inside the body to become misshapen, it only makes sense that there will be a pill to make it go back the other way. While I was thinking, I drew a picture of a mask crying with shapes and the headline, "Simplicity? Never." I wondered whether anyone would ever find the picture and analyze it after I died, like they do with the works of famous artists. There was nothing else for me to do but wait.

Simplicity Never

# Chapter Eleven
## Checking In

Before I knew it July 19th had arrived and I was being admitted into the hospital early for testing. Everything was checked, or let me put it this way, there wasn't anything that wasn't checked—my blood pressure, temperature, stomach sounds, urine, lungs, neck movement, reflexes, gait, height, weight, and even blood clotting (the doctors needed to know how long it would take me to stop bleeding, so they pricked my arm and sat with a timer to see how long it took for the bleeding to stop).

I hated the breathing tests the most. These were done to check my lungs to compare how I breathed before the operation with after. Some of the exercises were really easy. The one that checked my lung capacity looked like a kid's toy that I had to blow into and make the balls go up and down. I didn't like those tests much but they were a piece of cake compared to one that I found to be the most awful. For this one they placed a plastic tube in my mouth and then hooked the tube up to a machine. Then I had to inhale as much as I could until I heard a loud click, which startled me. It felt like I was suffocating because for a second or so I couldn't breathe in or out. Even though I knew I wasn't really suffocating, I found it scary. Since I couldn't swallow during this test, the drool just hung out of my mouth and fell in the napkins that were placed in my lap. I was very embarrassed but I was told that it would have been worse if I had braces on my teeth. Small consolation. I thought that there had to be a way of making these tests more comfortable and less degrading.

Once these tests were completed, the doctors were prepared for everything. They had pages and pages of information about me. They even examined the color of my fingers and nails so they would know what they should look like in case of emergency. I finally realized why I wasn't allowed to wear nail polish.

With all the testing finally finished, my doctor wrote down the last few pieces of information. It read: "Sixteen-year-old female, progressive thoracolumbar curve (57°) resistant to brace therapy for elective post fusion with CD instrumentation…iliac graft in AM."

Well, it was a done deal. I just wanted to go to my room and relax as much as I could. It was a very long day and I was tired. But first I had to be taken on a tour of all the rooms I would be staying in for the next week or so. They started to explain what would happen in each room, but I felt like saying, "No thanks." I made my parents listen. I didn't want to know any of the details. I preferred to be clueless and have it over already.

I can understand why some people want to know the exact details about what's going to happen, but not me. These are probably the same people who ask to have their operations videotaped so they can watch in the privacy of their own homes. No thanks. I'll pass… pass out?…probably!

# Checking In

Finally, after the grand tour, I went back to my room to watch TV. I was completely exhausted and my back was killing me. Dad went home to stay with my siblings so Grandma could take a break. Mom stayed with me while I got settled. In my room was another bed, for my roommate, Tery, but I didn't meet her that night. I saw her sneakers on the floor by the bed and the nurses told me about her. She couldn't walk and was having the same operation as I was to help her sit up straighter in her wheelchair.

While I was trying to relax in my room, I met Jed. He seemed nice, but he kept coming in and out of my room to visit.He said he was "over-ruled" because he was fifteen and I was sixteen and he was upset that he was no longer "the oldest patient on the fifth floor." I didn't know why this was so important to him and wondered how long he had been "on the fifth floor." I didn't wonder for long before he proudly told me that he had been in Newington Children's Hospital for six weeks and that this was his twenty-seventh time. I couldn't believe he was so happy about it.

I learned an important lesson from Jed. He made me realize that if people let their circumstances get them down, they'll be miserable. Instead, we need to make the best of the situation, no matter what. Seeing Jed smile at me made me realize that the most important thing is to be happy and never to give up. I thought that having scoliosis was the worst thing in the world until I met Jed. For the first time, I realized that scoliosis was never a life-threatening condition unless I let it affect how I lived my life. I thought that even though I had this terrible pain and an ugly bump on my back, I could still walk and run and do anything I wanted. Jed couldn't; he had no legs. Still, it didn't seem to make much of a difference to him. It was almost as if he didn't realize they were missing. He maneuvered himself around by using two different types of "transportation" he called it. Sometimes he came into my room on a small rolling table called a gurney that he lay on and operated with his arms. Sometimes he sped around in a really fast, compact wheelchair. The nurses were always yelling at him to stop racing down the hallways. He had so much fun making them mad and was always smiling. We talked for a little while and he left.

I watched TV and Mom went down the hall to use the phone. While she was gone, I met Max and Donny, two more visitors who wheeled themselves into my room. They were both about nine years old. Max just sat there in front of me a few inches from my bed. He didn't do anything but stare. Finally I said hi to him and he roared something back. Taken by surprise, I quickly turned to Donny, who was using his feet to move his wheelchair over to my bed. He had blue sneakers with Velcro straps and worn soles. Donny couldn't talk but he could hear. I hoped for a different response than the one I had gotten from Max when I finally got up the courage to say hi to him. In an instant he smiled, turned his wheelchair around, and immediately shuffled out the door, leaving Max behind. What had I said?

When my mother returned, Max was still sitting in front of me. I made a polite, wide-eyed introduction for the two of them. Luckily, he didn't roar this time. He didn't say or do anything; he just sat and stared. Mom asked him if he wanted to watch TV; still no response. So Mom and I watched television as Max sat in front of us and picked his nose.

Later that night, Mom and I had the room to ourselves and we played cards. Jed kept speeding in, saying something like, "What a resemblance," and then went speeding out again. Finally, within earshot, but not too close, he said I looked exactly like his old girlfriend. So that was what that was about: a crush.

It was late and I made Mom leave for the night. I knew she wouldn't be comfortable and besides, I didn't want her fussing over me and making me nervous. Surprisingly, I slept through the night.

Z Zz zZz zz zzz

# Chapter Twelve
## Zero Hour

Six o'clock in the morning came quickly and I was being awakened up by a large, gentle nurse. Yes, it was July 20th... already. She gave me a back massage with a disinfectant called Betadine. I was also given a Valium, which I didn't want to take. I was afraid to drink the water because I had been told I couldn't eat or drink anything after midnight and I didn't think I needed it. In the end, however, I did what I was told.

The sun eventually peeked through my window and it was time to get rolled down the hallway on a gurney. Was I nervous? No, I wasn't scared anymore because I had made up my mind and wanted to have it done. I also had had plenty of time to chicken out and the thought never crossed my mind. It wasn't until I was rolled down the hall into a tiny room that I started to get nervous. I began to shake, but I told the doctors and nurses that it was because I was cold. I really think I was. It was at that point that I was glad I had taken the Valium.

In the tiny room, miniature suction cups with wires were

glued onto my forehead, feet, and back. These were going to monitor my vital signs during the procedure. The strong, smelly glue was dried with a very loud air dryer. Then a hat that looked like Grandma's old hair dryer or a shower cap was put on my head and I was wheeled down more hallways to the operating room. On the way there I saw my parents. I had wondered when they would arrive. Of course, I didn't have a watch to tell the time. I could see they were looking at the wires and suction cups but they joked about the hat instead. I didn't laugh.

A minute later, after saying good-bye to my parents, I was whisked away down the hall and given a shot of anesthetic in my arm. Right before I fell asleep, I remember the assistant surgeon, Dr. Diana, asking me if I remembered "this guy." Of course I did. "This guy" was Dr. Renshaw, who had been treating my scoliosis for the last three years. I was happy to see him because I had complete confidence in him. He, too, commented on my hat. Then I was told to close my eyes and count backward from ten. I don't remember how far I got before I fell asleep. I didn't feel a thing. My parents waited for probably the longest several hours of their lives; they had to stay nearby or let the nurses know where they were at all times—the bathroom, the cafeteria, or out for a walk. They waited and waited and waited.

For those of you, like me, who do not like to hear the in-depth, technical details of an operation, please skip to Chapter Fourteen and I'll meet up with you there. For those who are brave enough to hear everything, read on. But *please* keep in mind that every case of scoliosis is different. This was my personal journey, it won't be exactly yours. Technology changes every day and has changed even in the time since I had experienced this. Each day brings new treatments as well as innovative surgical *and* non-surgical procedures. OK. I'll meet up with everyone at the chapter of your choice. See you there!

The
Operation

# Chapter Thirteen
# My Surgery ... in a nutshell

Welcome to the operating room (the OR). At this point in time I was already asleep, so without making this chapter too difficult with technical terms and medical language, here is what happened. After I fell asleep, I was rolled onto my stomach on a frame, so that I wouldn't be lying directly on the operating table but propped up under my chest and hips. My head rested on a pillow and my arms and legs were on soft supports. I was hooked up to machines that were connected to the suction cups with wires that I told you about earlier; these monitored my heartbeat and nerve function in the spine. There was also a machine that gave me back the blood I had stored at the Red Cross. At some point a tube was inserted so that I would be breathing in the anesthetic.

The first thing they did was to take match-like strips of bone from my hip. I would more accurately call it my butt because it was right above my left cheek, but technically it was my iliac crest. The strips were then put aside for use later. The area of the spine they started to work on began at my seventh thoracic vertebra, which is about the mid-shoulder-blade area **(see Figure 12)** and ended a few inches below my waistline.

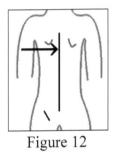

Figure 12

My muscles were pulled away from my spine and kept out of the way with metal clamps. Then each vertebra was opened up and all the tissue and ligaments were removed to expose the soft bone underneath. The hard bone from my hip was placed criss-cross on each soft bone of the vertebra for fusion. This meant that eventually all the bone strips would become one solid piece of bone. (This fusion process would take six to eight months, but I didn't even realize it was happening.)

Once the vertebrae, tissue, and ligaments were ready, the rods were inserted. Then the doctors used what I refer to as a car jack–type machine to straighten the rod as it was "propping up" my crooked spine. As the hooks along the rod were "distracted," my spine was straightened to less of a curve. Each click of the machine meant another degree closer to a nearly perfect spine. To make sure I was OK, I was rolled over and asked to wiggle my toes to make sure there was no paralysis. I don't remember any of this.

After the doctors decided everything was fine, I was put back to sleep and they continued to straighten me out a little bit more. When they were fully satisfied that my spine was as straight as possible for my degree of curve, they completed the operation. The rod was anchored securely with hooks, nuts, and bolts, and another rod was inserted. Then the nuts and bolts were tightened and filed down. After that I was basically hosed down with saline to make sure no metal pieces or shavings remained inside. Then the bone strips were packed under the rods to complete the fusion process. Some of this bone was mine but two ounces came from the bone bank, which I didn't know I would be getting. I was upset at first when I found out, but giving bone to myself before the procedure wasn't something I was prepared to undergo. Giving my blood was much easier. After everything was all set, my muscles were smoothed over my newly straightened spine and held in place with dissolvable stitches. Then my back was closed up beautifully and cosmetically from top to bottom, thanks to my surgeon. One tube needed to stay in my back for a while, but I couldn't feel it.

And that, my friends, in a nutshell, was my operation. I don't mean to minimize the magnificent talents of my surgeons, doctors, and nurses; not in the least. Without their expertise, I would still be crooked and in pain. Fortunately, that has changed, as you will soon see in Chapter Fourteen.

# "...the operation was a huge success and I didn't even feel a thing...,,

## Chapter Fourteen
## All Done!

Hi, again! Well, the operation was a huge success and I didn't even feel a thing. The doctors reduced my curve to 17°, which was minimal. It was about the same degree of curvature I had when the scoliosis was first diagnosed. Anyway, I basically made history for the hospital. They hadn't been able to get a curve of my magnitude down to such a minimal degree before.

I don't remember much about what happened right after the operation because I was in and out of sleep. I do, however, recall at one point waking up in a white room with a curtain and white machines around me. There were doctors standing on the far side of the room and when they saw me looking at them, they came right over to me. I recall lying on my back, trying to focus my eyes, but then I felt a soreness come over my body. The doctors told me I was fine and that I should go back to sleep, so I did.

The next time I woke up I was in Special Care, a place where I got all the undivided attention I wanted (and needed) from my own private nurses, who were in the room with me every single second of the day and night. They promised to care for me and not leave me alone.

It was here that I saw my parents for the first time since the operation. I was dozing off, but I remember watching my mother come in the door to see me. She covered her mouth and almost passed out, and wasn't able to enter the room. The nurses went out in the hallway to take care of her. So much for leaving me alone. Jeez. She could have pretended I looked good. Dad came over to see me. Although it took a lot of energy, I managed to whisper and ask him what was wrong. He told me that I had a lot of tubes and wires and things connected to me. I complained that I had something in my throat and couldn't swallow. I wasn't sure if it was phlegm or if my throat was really dry. Dad explained that what I was feeling was a tube that went in my nose and down my throat to my stomach to make sure no mucus got down there that would make me throw up. That was the last thing I needed. No wonder I couldn't swallow. I also had a tube in my back, which drained fluid, and I was still connected to the machines that monitored my heart, lungs, and vital signs. I also had an IV (intravenous line) in each arm, not to mention tubes so I could go to the bathroom. Luckily, I didn't really feel anything except my dry throat.

Mom made her way back into the room and the nurse offered to brush my teeth for me. I felt silly because I thought I could do it myself, so I said no. I soon realized that I couldn't do it myself, let alone have the energy to stay awake that long, so I let her brush; I needed it. I managed to lift my head just enough to spit into a plastic bowl. I found out later it was actually a plastic bedpan. Hey—as long as it was clean! Feeling secure with my parents and all my private nurses around, I fell asleep again. I don't remember when my parents left that night.

# All Done!

When I awoke, the nurses brushed my teeth for me again. Was it relaxing not to have to do anything on my own? No. There were really no restful moments after the operation. I was awakened every three hours for painkillers and I was "rolled" every two hours on the hour. I got sore lying in one position, especially when the anesthesia wore off, but when it came time for the nurses to roll me, I suddenly didn't want to change positions. After it was over, though, I felt much better, at least for a little while.

What was it like to be "rolled"? Well, two nurses came into my room and trust me, whenever I saw them, I knew why they were there. They told me to cross my arms on my chest while they took hold of both sides of the sheets under me. Then very slowly and gently they turned me from my back to my side using the sheets to move me. Once I was "rolled," the nurses propped me up with pillows behind my back and between my legs to relieve any pressure on my back. I was so glad when this was over, but it wasn't long before I was uncomfortable again.

At the next two-hour mark, like clockwork, two nurses again came into my room. This time I would be rolled onto my back. I was allowed to have one pillow under my head. The next time I was rolled onto the other side and propped up with pillows again. This continued—to the right side, to my back, to the left side, back—all week.

• • • • • • • • • • • • • • •

The next day I was taken out of Special Care and brought back to my old room on the fifth floor. I was lying down for the bumpy ride, still groggy and heavily medicated. When I got to my room, Tery's bed was still empty. I got worried because she had had the same operation as mine the day I checked in and I was back in our room before her. I was told that she'd had some complications in the OR. The operation should have taken six to seven hours; hers took ten, while mine was only four and a half. We think my procedure went quickly because I did all my exercises and stayed flexible. I was told she would be back in the room in a few days.

Over the course of the week and with the help of the physical therapists, I performed leg exercises. Since I couldn't move my legs myself, the therapist really did all the work for me for the first few sessions. Still, I was encouraged. I couldn't help thinking that I wasn't doing anything on my own. It was the same day that I was reintroduced to the breathing exercises I had learned during those pre-op tests. I had to breathe into the plastic toy and make the balls go up with each breath. I was supposed to beat my record from the previous day. It was so hard; I had no energy at all.

During the early days of my recovery, I was also reintroduced to the breathing exercise that I had hated the most when I checked in. It was the one where I had to inhale through a tube as the oxygen supply was cut off for a second. The loud click startled me every time it went on and off. It felt as if I was caught in the middle of breathing, like my lungs were being wrung out. It was too much for me to handle too soon. Being exhausted and frustrated, I started to cry and the exercise was taken away.

As for the pain: sometimes I would have my mother help me find the button to buzz the nurse to see if it was time for more medication. Most of the time it was only about thirty minutes since my last dose and I wasn't allowed to have more yet. It felt like forever before the nurses came in. Mom said the best thing I could do was to go to sleep to make the time go by faster between doses. So I did.

Every once in a while, when I dozed off, I would get nightmares that I was falling. I didn't feel like I was falling out of bed, but it seemed as if my arms and legs were too heavy to move. I felt like I was falling straight through the bed into a deep hole. I woke myself up in a panic a few times. It was really weird.

Speaking of weird: one night I was rolled on my side facing

away from the door. I woke up hearing a crunching noise near my bed. I waited and heard it again. Then I heard a crunch, a rustle of a bag, crunch, rustle…Someone was eating potato chips! I couldn't see who was there because I couldn't roll over without help yet. I asked who it was and a voice answered. She said she was a nurse from another floor. I was frustrated because I couldn't see her and I asked what she was doing in my room eating when I was still hooked up to IVs for food. I heard her throw the bag in my garbage and leave.

---

A couple days later all my tubes were out except one IV. The doctors said I could start having liquids. My first big meal was ice chips. Not ice cream; ice chips. I ate them very slowly. It felt good because they were so cold. Soon, I was able to eat a Popsicle. It was like a delicacy. It tasted good so I asked for another one. But after I ate them both, I got a stomachache. I felt bloated and I couldn't pass any gas or burp or anything. Maybe I should have only had one. As a result, the doctors took me off the liquid diet and it was back to the IV for food again. A minor bump in the road.

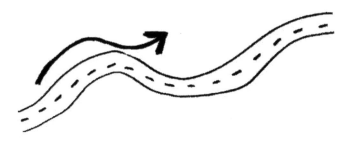

# Chapter Fifteen
# Baby Steps

It was nine days after the operation and the nurses informed me that I was going to get out of bed. I couldn't even roll over by myself, I thought, how was I supposed to get out of bed? I was scared. It was too soon. I wasn't ready.

I tried to refuse but the nurses came over to my bed and struggled as gently as they could to get me to sit up while keeping my body straight. That part was really painful. I felt like a baby. As I was being moved, something in my lower back started to tingle. At first I thought it was a muscle; then I got scared thinking it was the rod. But in a matter of seconds, I was sitting up all by myself. I was very happy.

Then the nurses informed me that it was time to go for a walk. What? Just as they started to help me out of bed, the assistant doctor came walking into my room. He was adorable and I had a crush on him, so when he said he would help, I was thrilled. He came over to me, put his hands under my arms, and literally lifted me up and sat me in the chair by my bed. I sat there for probably no longer than a minute before I was ready to lie back down. I felt nauseous and tired and I thought I was going to pass out. I ended up not going for a walk and I don't even remember returning to bed.

Each time the nurses got me up out of bed, I felt as if I was going to pass out. It didn't matter if I was going to sit up in the chair for a few minutes or go for a ride in the wheelchair to get X-rays; one time, I had to have some taken while I was standing and the nurses had to hold me up. I couldn't wait to get back in the wheelchair. Anyway, the X-rays looked good.

Before long, I started to be able to tolerate the pain in my back (which was gradually decreasing) until it was absolutely necessary to call the nurse. The doctors told me that this was a good sign; it meant that my back was healing. Eventually, I didn't need the morphine anymore and I was able to go back on the liquid diet and regular pain medicine.

Eventually, the rolling stopped and it was time for me to walk. Every couple hours I was helped out of bed, even if I wasn't ready. But each time I got up, I felt sick; they said I was working myself up. I was afraid of falling and my left leg didn't want to move so I had to drag it. My hip hurt where the bone had been taken for the fusion. It was as if I had to learn how to walk all over again. That first day I accomplished only a few steps.

The next day I walked around the hospital floor. It must have taken forever. I moved very slowly and carefully with the tightest grip on the arm of Linda, my nurse. This was the first time Mom saw me walking and she was very proud. Linda let Mom push the IV stand while the three of us inched our way down the hallway. I don't think my steps were even an inch long yet. It reminded me of that "Mother May I" game we used to play when we were kids in which we asked permission to take baby steps.

Plus, Mom was so afraid of pulling the IV out of my arm or making me trip that she kept making noises that made me really nervous and started to annoy me.

Somehow, we made it safely around the square-shaped fifth floor. I watched every step to make sure I had steady footing so I wouldn't trip. Linda kept telling me to pick up my left foot more instead of dragging it, but my hip was very sore. I was surprised I could move my leg at all. I think the hip hurt more than my back did. Eventually, we circled the whole floor and returned to my room.

All that exercise made me hungry. I actually hadn't eaten real food for nine days. I begged the doctor for some chicken broth and before he left he agreed to let me have a few teaspoonfuls. While Mom and I were waiting for my broth, she decided it would be a good time for her to go to the cafeteria and get some lunch. While she was gone, a nurse came in and I told her about the broth but she said she would have to check with the doctor. A while later she returned and said the first doctor had gone home so she brought in a new doctor, who said my stomach was still distended and I couldn't have the broth; then he left. I had been looking forward to the broth and when I couldn't have it, I started to cry. It was uncontrollable. I'm not sure why. The nurse saw how upset I was and said that it wasn't that she didn't believe me, but I was the patient and he was the doctor. I was very distraught but didn't have the energy to continue the conversation.

Finally, Mom came back from lunch and I burst out crying again. She got frantic thinking I was in pain until I told her the story. Soon Linda came in and we repeated the whole tale. About two hours later a nurse appeared with the chicken broth. I felt like saying I wasn't hungry anymore just out of spite.

Two days later (eleven days after the operation), Mom went home early; she was exhausted. I was glad she left because she needed the rest. Dad would be up to visit in a couple more days, but I hoped to be going home by then. Linda took me for another walk around the floor, but this time she didn't let me hold onto her. I was very scared but she assured me that she would be right there to help if I needed her. I was walking out of my room all by myself when Dad came toward me down the hall. What a surprise for both of us. I walked over to him slowly and proudly.

Dad stayed for a while and tactfully suggested that if I continued to walk around the hallways, I should put a T-shirt on underneath my dress. I was wearing a very loose-fitting lightweight cotton jumper. Even that much material bothered me because it pressed against my bandaged back. The annoyance was like sunburn, when you don't want anything to come near your sensitive skin. I put a T-shirt on under the jumper anyway, but it wasn't comfortable.

Before the IV was taken out, I received two pints of my own vitamin-enriched blood that was not used during the operation. It was refreshing, like a cold vitamin drink. I felt regenerated, like a new person. Someone remarked that the color returned to my cheeks. Finally, the nurses came in and took the IV out.

That night, after Dad left, Linda came into my room. I liked when she visited because she always had great stories. One night she told me that her five-year-old daughter wanted to know exactly how babies were made. She wasn't sure how or how much she should explain. When she was finished, her daughter said, "Well that explains it." Linda said her mouth dropped open. Apparently, her daughter had observed her pet rabbits doing "just that." We had a good laugh and I appreciated being treated like a teen, not like a child.

# "I couldn't believe how many little things are affected when your back is out of commission."

## Chapter Sixteen
## Making Progress

It was twelve days after the operation and I was able to get up and walk to the bathroom all by myself. Mom came into my room and when she saw I wasn't in bed, she got worried, but the nurses told her where I was. I tried to take my time and enjoy my privacy. Of course, everyone wanted to know if I was OK. While in there I slowly lifted my right arm to brush my teeth as I held the edge of the sink tightly with the other hand. I tried to breathe calmly so I wouldn't get worked up. I couldn't bend or lean forward to spit in the sink, so I spit in the plastic bowl instead. Actually, it was the bedpan again. When I was done, I was exhausted and needed help to get dressed. I couldn't believe how many little things are affected when your back is out of commission.

When I came out of the bathroom, the nurse told me to wait for her so she could be near me in case I tripped. Being independent and stubborn, I started walking anyway. Then I started walking faster.

The nurse screamed, "Wait, don't run!"

"I'm not," I said.

When I stopped and we all finished laughing, I explained that I had been holding onto the handle of the heavy bathroom door and as it was opening, it was pulling me with it. What a scary moment for all of us.

Once I calmed down, I noticed that my roommate, Tery, was watching kids' shows on TV. I was able to sit in the chair between our beds and stay awake from the beginning of *Zubilee Zoo* to the end of *Sesame Street*, a whole hour. I was very proud of myself.

Mom stayed until three o'clock but I told her to go home because she was tired and I was fine. After she left, we had a thunderstorm, which caused the electricity to go out. Fortunately, the hospital generator kicked in, but the TV had no power and there was absolutely nothing to do. Then I found out that there was a game room in the basement where kids could get together and play games. I wasn't sure if I felt like going.

An hour later, I made my way down the hall all by myself and used the phone to call my family. At first, they were scared that something had happened but I told them I decided to go downstairs to the "Rec. Room." The nurses got a wheelchair and sent for a messenger to wheel me down to the basement. I hated the ride; I felt every bump. We took an elevator that only hospital employees use. I felt uncomfortable being in the secluded elevator with this stranger, probably because I felt so helpless. I realized I was being ridiculous because the man who was wheeling me was a trusted employee of the hospital. Nonetheless, I was glad when the elevator stopped so we could get out.

When I got down to the game room, I saw the man who was in charge of getting all the kids together to play various games at different tables. I was wheeled to a table surrounded by other kids in wheelchairs with all kinds of problems: some couldn't speak clearly, some drooled, some had casts or braces on, some had missing fingers or hands. I thanked God that I had my hands, my brains, and my talents.

I ended up winning two games out of four, even though I could barely sit up in my wheelchair. By the last few games, I was in so much pain that I could barely lift my card onto the table. I would hold it out as much as I could and wait for the man to take it and put it on the table for me. I had just about enough energy to grasp the cards, but not enough energy to hold them upright. As a result, everyone at the table could see what I had in my hand. I felt like I was developmentally challenged but I didn't feel that anyone looked at me any differently. All the kids had some sort of problem to overcome. The difference was that mine would disappear in a very short time while their problems were not so easy to fix.

After the games, the man mentioned that I was smart and pretty and something about how I didn't look like there was anything wrong with me. Immediately, my stubborn side came out and with my last bit of energy I snapped back that there wasn't anything "wrong" with me and that he would feel this way too if he just had a spinal fusion. I wanted to go back to my room and I did.

The ride back was horrible. I held on tight over every bump. I kept thinking about how it didn't take much courage for me to escape to my room and how most kids who have problems that can't be fixed so easily have to face stupid people like him every day. I got back to my room and tried to get out of the wheelchair, but the driver hadn't locked the wheels, so it moved. He didn't help me either! I was ready for bed.

After he left, I lay down in bed for about a minute. A minute was just about all I could take because Tery was sick and I couldn't stand being in the room. Absolutely exhausted and sore, I got out of bed as quickly as I could. I carefully walked past the nurses at Tery's bed and down the hall. I called my parents to tell them about the UNO game. While I was standing at the phone, Dr. Diana walked by. He was so surprised to see me standing there all by myself. I was just as surprised to see him on his way to play video games in the kids' room. He said I could go home the next day as soon as I could prove I could walk up and down the stairs. I relayed the message to my parents on the phone. We were all very excited. It had been less than two weeks.

I could go home  the next day.

Slowly, I made my way back to my room. I was very tired and weak because I had stayed up for so long, but I couldn't wait for Linda to come in and talk with me. I liked listening to her stories. Her story that night was about a walk she had taken the day before. She had her music on and took a shortcut through the woods when she had a weird sensation. "Am I stupid to be walking through the woods alone with music on?" she thought to herself.

She walked out of the woods and noticed she was in a parking lot behind a school. Suddenly, out of nowhere, a car started speeding toward her. She could only think of how she would jump out of the way, to the left or to the right. As the car got closer, she realized it was a police car. The officer got out and asked her where she had just been. When she told him she was "in the woods," he asked if she had seen or heard anything. She hadn't. He told her that they were after a man in the woods wearing a mask. Then the officer got in his car and sped off, leaving her stranded in the middle of the school parking lot. She looked around and ran to the front of the school, where there were a bunch of police cars. She kept telling me how she could have been killed. I was thrilled that she shared such a story with me.

Linda was very emotional when I told her that I would be leaving the hospital the next day. She started to tear up and told me she would turn the light out because she felt silly. I didn't think so. Actually, I felt like she cared about me as a person, not as just another patient.

The next day I had to prove I could walk up and down one flight of stairs without help in order to go home. Who knew it would be so hard? I practiced with my nurse learning how to walk up and down stairs all over again. I couldn't lean backward too much or I would fall. I couldn't stand up straight or I would lose my balance. I had to remember to keep my body bent forward slightly, so if I tripped, at least I would fall forward and catch myself. The nurse kept reminding me to pick up both legs, not just go up and down on one leg. She told me not to move the other leg until I was sure that the first leg was planted steadily. I hoped no one noticed that I was hanging onto the banister for dear life. I thought it hurt to lift my leg just to walk down the hallway or do those exercises. I told myself to pretend it didn't hurt so that I could go home. And that's exactly what I did.

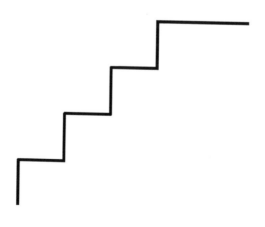

"I told myself to pretend it didn't hurt so that I could go home. And that's exactly what I did."

# Chapter Seventeen
# Homecoming

Time to go home at last. I was wheeled out of the hospital and helped by the nurses into our car, which was parked at the handicap ramp. They recommended that I put the thinner of the two pillows Mom brought with her behind my back to cushion the bumps. Of course I chose the thicker one. Fifteen minutes into the ride home, I decided I wanted the thinner, flatter pillow after all. Mom pulled over and we painstakingly switched pillows. Then back on the road again. Every time we hit a bump, I made a noise, which made Mom cringe. Soon Mom was driving so slowly it was ridiculous. And it didn't even help. I told her it might be better just to hurry home and get me out of the car already. My eyes were open wide the whole ride home, prepared for every bump that came along.

Almost an hour later, we finally pulled into our driveway. Once again, I couldn't get out of the car. But this time it didn't take a shove to help me. I didn't want anyone to come near. I emerged slowly and made my way past the two big bushes in front of my house, embarrassed to see balloons tied all over them.

81

Our dog, Cocoa, was locked in the kitchen behind the gate so he wouldn't jump and knock me over. When I got inside, I sat down on edge of the couch. Cocoa was let out and he sped out of the kitchen, peeled around the corner, and ran over to me. When he realized I wasn't going to sit on the floor and play with him, he calmed down, put his head in my lap, and looked up at me with sad eyes. He missed me.

It was my first day back home. We had steak and rice for dinner. I couldn't eat the steak because I wasn't used to chewing anything and my teeth hurt. After a few bites, I felt exhausted and decided it was time for more pain medication. I went upstairs to my bed and started writing in my journal about everything that had happened. I lay flat on my back and held the book up over me. (I felt like Michelangelo working on the Sistine Chapel.) It took every bit of energy to press the pencil against the paper to make it readable. Half the time I didn't have the energy to complete the sentences, so I only wrote, "Remind to tell about...."

The next day, a Saturday, I tried to watch a video but I couldn't sit up through the whole thing. Mom and Dad bought me a seat kind of like a kid's beach chair. Unfortunately, it was too low to the ground and I couldn't bend to get down that far. Who knew? I ended up sleeping most of the day instead.

Sunday I put my shorts on. It might not sound like much, but I was very proud. We had company over and ordered pizza, which I ate nibble by nibble. I had to drink my soda with a straw because my back hurt too much to lift the glass up to my mouth. More and more I was finding out what the back muscles were used for. After the pizza, I took a painkiller and went up to bed to write again. I was sure our company wouldn't mind.

Monday, three days after I got home, I was still taking sponge baths from the sink to avoid wetting the bandages. Changing them was quite challenging. The tape that held the bandages on had to be ripped off. I swore that it felt like they were stuck on with electrical tape. The worst part about it was that the tape ran all the way up and down each side of my back. Thank God this was the last day because taking it off was a huge ritual. I stood in the bathroom with my shirt off and a towel covering my front. Then Mom and Dad grabbed hold of the tape and start pulling, slowly, while I just stood there cringing.

I really don't know how they did it at all. They certainly went through a lot more than they had been given credit for over the years. Who knew that at the age of sixteen I would need them to change my bandages.

For the next two days, nothing exciting happened, I just felt mopey.

Thursday, six days after I returned home, was a pretty exciting day. I had a burst of energy and took my first shower. All of a sudden I felt too independent to have my mother help me get undressed, although I did want her to help me get in the shower. I had trouble lifting my leg over the side of the tub and I was afraid of falling. Once I got in and she left, I closed the shower curtain, got undressed, and threw my clothes out onto the floor. It felt so good. I was scared that the shampoo or soap would sting my scar or that water would hurt as it came down, so at first I stood out of the way of the stream. Little by little, I moved closer and didn't even feel the water dripping on my back. I was able to take a normal shower. I even turned around to have the water beat directly on my back; it felt great.

As if taking my first shower wasn't eventful enough for one day, then I started to laugh uncontrollably. Wow, it hurt! I've never been able to laugh a little laugh. If someone gets me going, I can't stop. Once I was timed laughing for eight minutes straight, no joke!

83

My cousin J. could always make me laugh with just a wiggle of his finger from across the room. My cousin Kevin could mimic the way I laugh when I'm trying to stop laughing and that gets me going even more. He's fun. We've been close since we were toddlers pulling each other around in the wagon.

Anyway, the reason I started laughing, I told my sister I had diarrhea so bad that it burned. She thought I said that it was burning a hole through my pants and for some reason we couldn't stop laughing. That threw my back into a spasm. I lay on my parents' bed and laughed and cried for at least four minutes. I laughed and screamed in pain at the same time, but I couldn't stop laughing. Mom started to yell because she didn't know what else to do to help and that made me laugh even more. She said I was scaring her. Scaring her? I was scaring myself. I just couldn't help it. Every time I thought I was ready to stop, I would burst out laughing again. Mom said it was "a great release of a lot of tension."

The next day was Friday and everyone was leaving for a trip to Maine. Everyone ... except me. We had booked the cottage the previous year and we had thought I would be able to go and relax. Unfortunately, I didn't want to go near the car, let alone sit in it for five hours between sleeping bags, travel games, pillows, elbows, and each sibling's invisible, uncrossable line. No thanks. I was looking forward to the peace and quiet. So here it was five in the morning, a week after I returned home from my operation. My family was packing up the car. They almost decided to stay home with me, but I made them go. I didn't want them around fussing over me and missing their vacation. An hour and a half later I was bored and couldn't wait for them to return home. Of course, I wouldn't tell them that.

Later that morning Grandma came over to stay with me. What an experience that was to be!

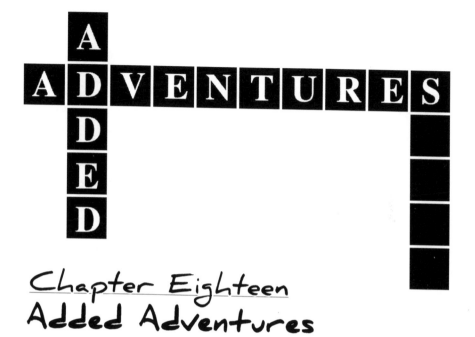

# Chapter Eighteen
## Added Adventures

For the next week Grandma stayed with me. And what a memorable week it was.

I awoke the next morning, Saturday, and went downstairs to what felt like a sauna. I couldn't breathe because the air was so heavy. Grandma had opened the door to the air-conditioner and insisted that "some breeze was coming through." She didn't know how to turn it on and she hadn't opened any windows.

That week I tried to teach Grandma how to use the TV remote control, but my efforts were useless. She wanted to watch a black-and-white Western movie that bored me out of my mind. I don't like using the word "bored" because Mom says that "only boring people get bored," but I was really bored. There was no other word for it. I went upstairs to write in my journal but fell asleep instead.

The next day, Grandma insisted on washing the dishes instead of putting them in the dishwasher. Once I taught her how to use it, I thought we were getting somewhere. Then I noticed that she washed all the dishes *before* she put them in the dishwasher.

It was five am, ten days after I had come home from my operation and the phone began ringing. I could barely walk, but I jumped out of bed, almost hurting myself. Grandma was trying to answer the phone without pressing the talk button. I grabbed the phone away from her and answered without looking at the number. All I heard was a slow, deep male voice whispering, "Hhhiii hhhowww hhhare hhhyooouuuu?" Shivers went up and down my body and I quickly ended the call and turned the ringer off .

I told Grandma what happened, got back in bed, and pulled the covers over my head, trying not to be scared. What would ever possess someone to call like that? Get to bed or get a life you weirdo. Then I got worried that he knew where I lived, who I was, and that I was alone in the house with my grandmother. I finally fell asleep when I heard Grandma snoring.

Z Z z Z zzZ zz     Z Z z zZ zzZ z.Z zz

It was Tuesday, eleven days after I had come home from the hospital and what a great day it was. It was cool outside and for some reason that made my back feel better. I was able to put on long pants all by myself. Then I progressed to the biggest accomplishment of the day—getting my socks on. It doesn't sound like a big deal, but it was. First, I had to figure out a way to bend so that I could open the drawer. I stood in front of the dresser drawers for a few minutes debating whether my feet were really that cold; they were. The next debate I had was whether or not I had the energy to take on such a project. I decided that I was up for the challenge ... and I had nothing else to do.

I bent down (as if I was wearing a back brace) using my legs and keeping my knees bent. At this point I was kneeling next to the drawer, staring at it. I wasn't sure why I did this; it wasn't like it would magically open up all by itself. I couldn't believe what little thought and strength it had taken to open the drawer before the operation; now it took lots of self-encouragement and every bit of strength I had in me. But I did it: I opened the sock drawer...and then...it was time to put the socks on.

I don't know how I put them on that day, but somehow I did. I sat on the edge of the bed and dangled one sock out in front of me. I could neither bend nor put my foot on my lap so I stretched my arm out as far as I could toward my foot. I managed to get my big toe into the opening of the sock and by crunching all my toes together I put it on. It was a major accomplishment. The only decision left was whether I wanted to walk around with one sock on all day or attempt to put the other one on, too. Well, I did it.

I was very happy. If you want something badly enough you will do anything in your power to do it, get it, accomplish it, or have it. I took a nap soon after that because I had tired myself out.

Although she could have popped our food into the microwave, Grandma preferred cooking it the long way. I guess it's hard to break old habits. Whenever I put anything in the microwave, she told me that I had to keep it in longer because it wasn't warm yet. I tried to explain the microwave to her but I didn't have the energy, so I assured her it was warm enough, ate, and went to lie down.

It was Wednesday, the twelfth day home, and that morning (and the night before) were the first times since the operation that I could brush my teeth and actually bend a little to spit into the sink. By this time I had gained the energy to cup my hands together, fill them with water, and lift it to my mouth. I compare the feeling of not being able to do it, to being young. Remember when you were little and you didn't have the coordination to cup your hands together but you still tried and the water spilled out? That was how I felt.

That day Grandma was throwing a tennis ball to Cocoa in the house. He was very happy; he kept running around the dining-room table and returning to the living room for another toss. One time the ball hit the TV screen and Grandma said the "roughhousing" had to stop. (And she was the one doing it.) It was funny to see her playing with Cocoa because at first she wouldn't even go near him.

That night, I was able to stay up and watch two complete shows on TV. Afterwards I still felt fine so Grandma and I decided to play cards but first we had to turn on the light over the dining-room table, and we were both too short to reach it. The only way to do it was to stand on a chair and kneel on the edge of the table and neither of us was about to do that. I went into the living room and tried to drag the floor lamp over. This probably wasn't a smart move because the lamp was a little heavy. The cord ended up being too short and the outlet too far away, but it was better than having no light at all. We played a few games until I got tired.

The next day, my thirteenth back home, I noticed that all the balloons my family and friends brought me were floating half-mast around the room and the flowers were dying. The only survivors were the cactus from my aunt and uncle and the stuffed animal from my parents. His arms were raised and his shirt said, "Why me?" It was so appropriate.

Each day brought new accomplishments and new things that I wanted to do or try. I sat on the floor for the first time since the operation. I bent my knees as if I had a brace on and bent all the way down until my knees touched the floor. Then I leaned over to one side, the same way I was taught to get out of bed. Cocoa was so happy that he came right over to me and I rubbed his tummy. He was just glad that I was paying attention to him. I spent the day lounging around; I felt tired and lazy.

The next day, Friday, was two weeks since I had come home and one week that my family had been away. Grandma and I left Cocoa in the kitchen at night behind the gate so we wouldn't trip over him. In the morning, though, the gate blocked me from going to eat breakfast. It was hard for me to unlock because I couldn't touch it unless I bent my knees. Then I had to grab the wooden bar that locked the gate in place and pull it upward. I didn't have the strength to do this or the energy to explain it to Grandma so I decided to go over the fence. Somehow, I successfully managed to get one leg over. At this point I was standing with one leg in the kitchen, one in the dining room, with the gate in between them. I tried to get the other leg over without Grandma hearing me; eventually I made it. When I was done sneaking around the kitchen, I made my way back over the gate. The next thing I heard was Grandma squealing and lecturing me about hurting myself. She scared me half to death and I tried not to wobble over. She gave me one of her famous love taps on my butt. It hurt a lot but I couldn't tell her that she hit right on the spot where my hipbone was healing. She won. I didn't climb over the gate again.

That day I ate nearly nonstop. I don't know why I was so hungry. Unfortunately, Grandma had decided to cover every single thing in the refrigerator with tin foil. In order for me to see what was in there, I had to lean into the refrigerator and open everything up. Wasn't that in a movie once?

Later that night I was in the kitchen taking my medicine. Grandma decided to go to bed. She flipped the light switch at the bottom of the stairs, which was actually the switch for the kitchen, not the stairway. So I was standing in complete darkness, afraid to move and trip over Cocoa. When I flipped the switch on, Grandma flipped hers again, and the darkness returned. We finally figured out what was happening and I walked quickly into the other room while the light was on to explain the setup to her and show her where the switch for the stairway was.

Soon we were off to a peaceful night's sleep until Cocoa woke us up barking. He never barked at night, even during thunderstorms when he was a puppy. I got really scared. It sounded as if he had sucked in all the air possible and blasted it out as loud as he could. Anyone would have thought he was three hundred pounds instead of thirty. I went downstairs as quickly as I could and flipped the switch at the bottom of the stairs for the kitchen. Then I just waited, too scared to move. I hoped that the light from the kitchen would scare away anyone who might be at the door. My heart was pounding in my chest and in my throat. After Cocoa calmed down, I looked out the windows and didn't see or hear anything, so we all went back to bed. In the morning we found out that an animal had ripped apart our garbage and scattered it all over the yard. I couldn't bend to pick it up and Grandma had a difficult time. What a week!

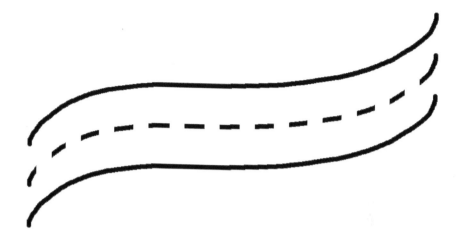

# Chapter Nineteen
## The Road to Recovery

It was fifteen days since I had come home from the hospital and everything was going well. My family was coming home from vacation and I couldn't wait to see them. I knew they would be surprised by how much I had progressed.

As soon as my family came in the door, I dropped an earring on the floor and bent down really fast to pick it up, so fast that I even scared myself. Of course, I didn't let them know. I just wanted to show them how far I had come and how much they had missed.

I still wasn't allowed to lift anything. But feeling better and forgetting that I hadn't lifted anything heavier than a glass of juice in a while, I lifted a very heavy bowl of pasta from the fridge. I nearly dropped it because it was heavier than I thought. My back started to tingle and burn in a certain spot but I didn't want to tell anyone I had lifted anything. After a while, my back still hurt and I started to wonder what could be wrong. I didn't know why it was burning. I started to worry that the rod had broken or something. We went all the way back up to Newington Children's Hospital for

X-rays. I guess that when I lifted the bowl I had aggravated the muscles that were trying to heal around the spine, pulling them, and now they had to heal back again. I felt much better knowing that the rod was not broken. Besides, I was told that it would take a lot more than just lifting a bowl to break the stainless steel rod or yank it away from the spine. We all felt better and drove home.

• • •

My friend Marifrances came to visit. I thanked her for the long letters that she had written to me while I was in the hospital, which had given me something to look forward to. I also realized who my good friends were and that it didn't matter how many I had so long as there were a couple of unwavering ones.

When friends did come to visit me at home, I didn't want them to sit on the edge of my bed because the movement of the mattress made me feel uncomfortable. When I was sitting on the couch, I didn't want anyone to sit next to me because the cushions would tilt and I would start to topple over in their direction. It got to the point that no one wanted to sit near me at all. No matter how softly they sat down, I would make a face and cringe with little noises that made everyone around me nuts. My family eventually banned me from the couch because everyone was tired of sitting still and not being able to move, sitting on the far end from me, or sitting on the floor to please me. So I turned to writing in my journal pad again.

Soon it was mid-August, a month since my operation. I hadn't gone out much because of the heat. Then Mom announced that I was going to church. It was one of my first times out. It was hot in church; I thought I was going to pass out. I was sitting up very straight because the backs of the pews were hard and curved, so I couldn't really lean back. When it was time to go to Communion, I walked slower than any old person in the whole church. It wasn't that my back hurt; I was afraid I would trip.

# The Road to Recovery

I felt that I could stand straight and rigid with my "new spine." Well, of course I was straighter, but I felt awkward about it and thought it was more noticeable than it really was. When I got in the car, I had a weird feeling in my back. I felt as if it was oozing. I got worried that my scar was bleeding. Even though I knew this wasn't possible, I had Mom check it anyway. I was still too afraid to look myself. For some reason I thought the incision would look like railroad tracks. Mom said everything was fine but we called the doctor to make sure. He said that everything was healing and that was what I had been feeling. I didn't think I was ready to get out that weekend but I was glad I did because school would be starting soon and I needed the practice of leaving the house.

Mom, Dad, and I had been taking walks around the neighborhood. As the days went on, I walked faster, regained more energy, and felt less pain. On one of our walks, we were in the middle of the street and a car came along. Mom and Dad hurried across the street, forgetting that I couldn't keep up. It must have been a funny sight to see me half walking, half shuffling to get across the street without hurting myself. We couldn't stop laughing. There are so many little things that we take for granted every day.

One of those little things was doing laundry. Wet clothing seemed so heavy to me. Not only that, the wet clothing from the washing machine was all bunched up and entwined. I found a way to empty the washing machine...one piece of clothing at a time. I had just about enough energy to reach in and pull on something. If that piece didn't budge, I started to pull on something else. Eventually, I would find a piece that I could pull out, a single sock or something like that. So I would walk over to the dryer, put the sock in, and return to the washing machine for another try, as if something had moved while I was gone. What felt like ten hours later when I finally finished, there was always that one lonely sock in the bottom of the machine that I couldn't reach without bending over and hurting myself. That one could go around for another wash. Oh, and forget about the one that fell on the floor. It was staying there. I didn't need it cleaned this time around anyway.

Another adventure was filling a pot of water or the teakettle for Grandma. I heard of the saying about the watched pot, but I wondered what the saying would be if the pot is filled one cup at a time. That's what I tried but I still had the problem of lifting the pot from the sink to the stove. I discovered something that probably wouldn't have made Mom happy. I pulled the sink sprayer as far as it would reach to the stove and hoped that the water landed in the pot so I didn't have to lift it or clean up. Hey, it worked!

Also, going to the bathroom during recovery wasn't easy. First, I had to bend to sit on the toilet. Then I had to twist to reach the toilet paper. I mustn't forget to mention the back muscles involved in the whole process, but that's enough of that.

I was looking forward to school starting, although I wasn't sure I was physically ready to go back.

# Chapter Twenty
# 'Back' to School

It was a month and a half since my operation and time to go back to school. I bet no one else had as exciting a summer as I did. At last I got up the courage to look at my back; I was very scared. When I finally did peek, I was pleasantly surprised. The scar just looked like a thin, straight, pink line. It wasn't gross-looking at all. I was greatly relieved.

Before school resumed I started having nightmares that people would be so excited to see me that they would rush up and try to hug me and hurt me without realizing what I had been through. I quickly developed what I called "the hand," before "the hand" became popular. Whenever I saw someone I thought might come up to me, I put out my hand to stop them.

As I was preparing for the start of school, I tried on my uniform skirt and realized that it was hemmed crooked to compensate for the curve from when I had scoliosis. I love saying that, "when I HAD scoliosis." What a great feeling it was to have the hemline straightened because my body was now straightened.

Every day I became more confident about how I looked. I especially loved how I could tuck in my shirts and have a perfectly normal waistline. I had lived with scoliosis for almost seven years. I couldn't believe I hadn't had the operation sooner.

When I returned to school, I was able to get special passes that let me get out of class a few minutes early so I could get to my locker and retrieve my book for the next class. That meant that I didn't have to carry anything too heavy and I didn't get caught in the rush when it was time to change classes. I was so afraid of being bumped in the back or pushed that I had the "don't come near me" look for the first few weeks.

Eventually, I got more comfortable and I didn't have to go to the nurse's office for Tylenol to get through the day. I also got more comfortable and less rigid walking with my "new spine," as I liked to call it. Although I never wore braces on my teeth, I liked to use the analogy. At first, when your teeth are straightened, they hurt a lot. In time, the tension eases up. That was how it felt to me, and like the pressure and pain involved with braces, the tension eased up on my spine, too.

At my three-month checkup the X-rays showed that my curve had leveled at 20°. I was still convinced that the tiny spot where the bone was taken from my hip hurt more than my back. I was told that the feeling is comparable to what a healing bone feels like after it's broken. Fortunately, I had never had a broken bone.

It was my senior year of high school and I decided that I would have a good time and get involved in everything I possibly could. Since I wasn't able to go to dancing school for a while, I took art class, choir, creative writing, and continued the extra-curricular activities from the year before. I was both very busy and very happy.

Three months after my operation I went with my senior class to Washington, D.C., for our class trip. I didn't tell anyone, especially my parents, but I didn't prepare myself adequately for the trip. I really didn't know what to expect. I wanted to go so badly and even though I had a great time, I paid the price. First, there was the bus ride from Connecticut to Washington. I called my parents when I got there and lied that I was fine. The truth was that I felt every bump. It was nothing compared to the ride home from the hospital, of course, but I was determined to have a good time no matter what. Being able to join my classmates on this trip was one of the things I was concerned about before I even decided to have the operation.

The second part about not being prepared was that there was a lot of fast walking in order to keep up with everyone in the group. There were guided tours and I struggled to keep up the pace. By this time I had been practicing walking around the neighborhood with my parents, but we didn't walk fast because I got too tired. While visiting Georgetown, I experienced de´ja` vu . A huge group of us was crossing the street and all of a sudden cars and buses started speeding toward us. You know what happened next? Yes, they all ran across the street, leaving me behind. Once again, we couldn't stop laughing.

Finally, there was the sleeping situation; four girls to a room, two per bed. I felt every movement whenever my bedmate tossed or turned. Then I rolled over onto my stomach and she flopped her arm right across my back. Wow! Enough said.

Throughout the trip I pretended that I felt fine and even found a comfortable position on the bus ride home. I kneeled on my seat, facing backward, talking to friends in the seats behind me. My back wasn't pressed against the back of the chair so I didn't feel the bumps as much. It wasn't until a few months later that I told my parents how I really felt on the trip.

\* \* \*

My senior year just flew by. I was able to twist my body a little and drive the car again. I kept busy and happy with all my activities. I even managed to earn a place on the honor roll. I became more and more confident every day. I started feeling that I was somewhat attractive and I even stepped out of my comfort zone and started dating, which helped boost my self-esteem. It's so weird that when you don't have anyone special in your life, you can't buy a date, but when you finally meet someone worth considering, suddenly everyone wants to "get to know you better."

As the year went on, I was recovering just fine. I got stronger and less worried about people bumping into me or touching my back. Then, in March, eight months after my operation, I visited Newington Children's Hospital again on an emergency visit. I had fallen down the stairs. Actually, I slipped down about five steps, but was able to grab hold of the railing. I felt like I was yanked back and my lower back started to hurt and tingle and burn. I thought something shifted, as if the rod had become disconnected, but the X-rays showed that "the instrumentation was intact."

Two months later, ten months after my operation, I got a part in the spring musical. I didn't tell my parents what I would be doing because I didn't want them to tell me that I couldn't. When they came to see the play, they were cringing in their seats as I ran around on stage. I felt fine.

My senior prom was approaching, and it was time to go shopping for a dress. I found a strapless dress that showed a little of my scar at the top, but I really liked it so I bought it. Yes, I finally had the courage to wear something that revealed my scar. The prom was eleven months after my operation and my scar looked like a thin line, as if I took my fingernail and scratched my arm really lightly. I was thrilled that throughout the whole night no one even noticed it. Besides, my date complimented me on how I looked and that was all that mattered. It was the first time since the operation that I wore heels. It felt a little funny to walk in them and keep a relaxed posture. We danced almost all night. I didn't do any crazy moves but had a great time. We went to an after party and I felt fine.

Graduation wasn't far behind. I received an award and graduated with honors. I was very happy and couldn't wait to go to college. Most important, I was so glad I didn't have to worry about my back anymore. It was summer and I didn't have to wear a brace or hide a bump. I even went out and bought a two-piece bathing suit. For the first time ever, I had a perfect waist, even hips, and a flat back. What a great feeling that was. I didn't even care that my scar was showing. It had already started to fade so no one even noticed. I would recommend the thin line over the "bump" any day.

# Chapter Twenty-One
# I Can Do Anything

That summer, one year after my operation, I was acting in a play at night and had my very first waitressing job during the day, lifting trays of food and bins of dirty dishes, and scooping ice cream, which wasn't as easy as it looked. I gained muscles that summer and I think it helped my back get stronger. It certainly was another challenge to overcome before college. (I gained confidence, too.)

And confident is what I became. Through all these experiences I had developed a stronger sense of independence. I tried new things and I knew what I liked to do and what I could do without. I also learned that I couldn't just sit home and do nothing because I was afraid of what "might happen." What "might happen" to me "might happen" to anybody, with or without rods in their back. I just had to use my head and go out and have fun.

Although the recovery process was long, it was well worth it. I can honestly say I became a different person. Suddenly I was standing straight, not lopsided. My clothes fit perfectly because my back was flat, not protruding. My spine was strong, not dependent on the brace to hold it up, and that constant throbbing pain was gone. Finally, I had no prickly heat, no bump, no everyday pain, no humiliation, no anger, no frustration, no sweaty undershirts, no skirts to be hemmed, no rawness, no redness, no Velcro! I was the happiest I had ever been. I finally had the perfect waist and an even waistline, one that I had only dreamed of before. I know it must sound silly. You don't realize what you have until it is taken away from you. In my case, when I was old enough to develop a nice figure, I couldn't, which made me want it even more. Finally I felt great. I could do whatever I wanted, except horseback riding because the bumps would be too jarring on my back. Oh, and I wouldn't recommend bungee jumping either, but everything else should be fine and pain-free.

••••

Soon I was off to college and what an experience it was, but that's another book entirely. Anyway, because I was sleeping in a strange new bed during the first few days, I couldn't walk. My back was very sore and stiff. What helped was buying orthopaedic egg crates for my bed, the foam layer that goes over the mattress and under the sheet and looks like fingers. As soon as I put that on my bed, my back felt wonderful. Pretty soon everyone who sat on my bed had to have one for theirs. It kept the mattress from feeling like it was slanting and grooving and it felt much softer and more comfortable.

One year and five months after the operation I went ice skating for the first time in my life. My parents knew I was going and Mom kept saying she didn't think it was a good idea, but I went anyway. I thought that anyone without rods could get hurt just as easily as I could (although I didn't have any intention of getting hurt). I had my mind set that I wasn't going to fall.

I made my way into the rink. With each circle around the rink, I became less stiff. I was able to relax because after a few times around by myself, I knew I wasn't going to fall. Then, on my last time around, out of nowhere, someone came up behind me and lifted me off the ground by my elbows. I knew it was a male but I didn't know who. We were going really fast. He didn't say anything. I couldn't see him. Then I heard the voice; it wasn't anyone I knew. I was in his way and instead of skating around me, he skated through me and we both fell. I couldn't believe it. I was doing so well and this idiot had to plow right through me. I also couldn't believe that my back didn't get hurt, only my elbows from hitting the ice. That was my last time ice skating.

Back in college, I had a great semester and never wanted to go home. For spring break I stayed at school and had a great time. We all got bad sunburns but had a blast. I even played air volleyball. It was the big cage-like thing that you see at carnivals with a big balloon to jump on and a net that separated the sides. We had a huge ball that we tried to hit back and forth over the net as we were jumping up and down in our socks. It didn't bother my back at all. My parents couldn't believe it when I proudly blurted out my new accomplishment.

At that point they shouldn't have been surprised at anything. Once I wrote them a note from school saying that I went sky-diving, which I really didn't do and probably never will. Then, in small print on the bottom, I wrote that I was just kidding. They didn't see the kidding part before I got the phone call.

With each new thing I attempted, my parents just had to deal with it and accept it. Scoliosis patients know what they can and cannot handle and will protect their backs at all costs. So my advice to parents is not to worry. My parents cringed every time I told them about something new. I learned to tell them after the fact.

The summer after my freshman year I learned how to play tennis. I had never even held a racket before. I found that as the as the minutes went on, my back got tired and sore from the twisting movement. Unconsciously, I started to hold the racket funny, tensing my body so that I didn't have to twist so much. When I got cranky we knew it was time for a break. Staying in shape was definitely something I needed to do. I couldn't depend on the rods to keep me standing straight. I still needed strong muscles to help the rods do their job.

It was a productive summer. I was cast in the operetta The Pirates of Penzance and got hiked over the pirates' shoulders like sacks of potatoes, kicking and resisting across the stage. It was a lot of fun. My parents still cringed in the audience but I was fine. I could do anything.

And that was just what I did. I even went to a theme park and on a roller-coaster ride. If I was going to go at all, I should have picked a better one because it was too bumpy and jarring. I never told anyone but I was scared out of my mind. I was getting pushed around so much. I kept having visions that my rod would get pulled right off my spine. What was I thinking? I won't be going on another one of those. Luckily, I didn't get hurt.

Over the next year I learned how to ski, ride a wave runner, and rollerblade. I like skiing the best. I was terrified the first few times because I was so afraid of falling. I snowplowed and stayed stiff almost the whole time. This was very tiring. Eventually I got more courage and realized that the snow was soft to fall on and my back relaxed a little bit more. I even fell on a big patch of ice without doing any damage.

And that's it. I'm proud to say the rest is history. Mostly, I'm just having fun, running around without a bump on my back or a brace under my clothes, not a care in the world. The most important advice I can give is to stay in shape. My back gets sore when it is not in shape, perhaps because I am depending on the rods to keep me straight. So even though I don't have any mandatory exercises to do, I still need to do something. I like to do stomach crunches but can't do a full sit-up very well. Besides that, all is normal. Sometimes I can predict a weather change, like rain or snow, but I can live with that and a couple of Tylenols once in a while. It's nothing compared to what it used to be.

A common question people ask is about having children after a spinal fusion. My answer to that is that I'm as normal as can be. I just might need extra medical supervision. Another question is if the rods will ever be taken out. I always respond, "Now why would I want to do that? I don't want to go through that again. Once was enough." Seriously, I love my rods. They helped boost my self-esteem and bring out the person I am today, the one that was hidden for so long. And what a journey that was!

# Some Advice

Make sure you keep yourself busy with plenty of activities to keep your mind off of moping and self-pity. Puberty is stressful enough without having to worry about scoliosis, too. Exercises keep the back from being dependent on the brace or the rods, so do them. Be open with your doctors and find out the best ways to handle each situation. Learn from my experiences and find the best ways to handle your life with scoliosis. Research the options available; medical technology is always changing and improving. Be as positive as possible and keep a journal or diary to help sort out your emotions and thoughts. Don't stand in the way of your dreams. You can do anything as long as you don't let the curvature get you down. Realize that most people don't understand scoliosis. How can they? And most importantly, know that you and your family are not alone. Good luck!

# About the Author

© 2002 Tracy Weed

I overcame many obstacles on my scoliosis journey. I attribute getting through it to the help of my family and writing in my diary. I'm glad I had the surgery and most of all, I love to refer to my scoliosis in the past tense. This was a photo of me when I first wrote and published this book.

While obtaining a Bachelor of Science degree in Corporate Communication and a minor in Graphic Design at Southern Connecticut State University, I became Grandma's primary caregiver. My time with her was a quirky, unpredictable gift. She eventually received the devastating diagnosis of Alzheimers. It will be my next book called *Lost Memories, Found Hope.* Coming Soon!

During part of that time, I enjoyed painting, and performing in musicals. I became a requested wedding vocalist throughout CT and NY. I would write children's books, poetry, or song lyrics in my spare time.

Then, *life happened …*

# Updates for You

I married in 2005, and I am a proud mom to Kaitlyn Hope and Brendan Joseph.

Absolutely convinced that my next book would be a sequel to *Growing Up with Scoliosis*, I thought I would have back pain and terrible experiences with pregnancy. I was ready to write about every moment of it, but my back felt great, so "uneventful" meant I had nothing to write about. I'm pleased to be able to update everyone about that now.

I'm proud to announce that *Growing Up with Scoliosis* has helped thousands of scoliosis families nationwide. I love sharing my updates and being an inspiration.

© 2008 Michelle Spray

# Updates for You

I'm pleased to know that I am helping to so many beautiful and strong young women and their families. Here I am with the Connecticut Chapter of Curvy Girls @CGScoliosisCT

# Updates for You

I divorced in 2009 even though both my children developed "additional needs" requiring countless surgeries, procedures, and specialists. It was a long journey and I'm considering how I want to write about it.

# Updates for You

In 2013, I met the love of my life, Erick, and his two children, Daniel and Abby. We got married in 2016 and blended our 6-person family seamlessly. Now they want a dog. Thank you Erick for always putting me first and for being my biggest cheerleader! I love you ... Forever.

# Updates for You

Order a copy *or two* of **My Journal, My Life** so you can **write your own story.** This journal contains 120 lined pages without dates so you can begin your story from the past or in real-time. Yours can be the next scoliosis book! www.amazon.com

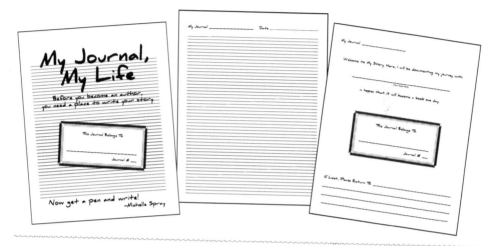

## Other books by Michelle Spray
*My ABCs* (An ABC Book for Any Age) and *Fidget and Scoot Discover the Rainbow!* www.amazon.com/author/michellespray

*Coloring Book versions of *My ABCs* and *Fidget and Scoot* are coming soon! To be updated when these books are available, please subscribe to the e-mail list: www.michellespraybooks.com/updates

# Testimonials

Michelle Spray started a diary to record her feelings when she was diagnosed with scoliosis in the fifth grade. The diary continued through her brace therapy to a spinal fusion done in the summer of her junior year of high school. The entries relate not only Michelle's feelings but also those of her parents and siblings. The last part tells of her elation at the success of her back surgery. To be diagnosed with scoliosis and watch the progression clearly is horrendous; but this little book will give courage to anyone with scoliosis and should be in every school library.
-Barbara Jo McKee, Printed in KLIATT Magazine, 09/02

Growing Up with Scoliosis is most certainly a wonderful story which takes you through days in the life of a young girl's emotions and physical being while dealing with Scoliosis. As a young girl myself growing up with Scoliosis, I enjoyed reading this story. I could relate to many of the author's trials and tribulations that she details so throughly in this book. Her positive outlook, words of wisdom and motivation are truly inspirational!
-Debbie Baierlein, The Scoliosis Association

Spray's adolescence was a study in scoliosis. Now a beautiful, young college grad with multiple talents, a straight back, and a normal body shape, she is in a perfect position to have written this upbeat and uplifting memoir. Diagnosed during a fifth-grade screening, Michelle reacted with predictable anger, denial, and resentment. As she grew, the curve-despite increasingly intense forms of bracing-worsened, and she eventually had to undergo a complex spinal fusion. Her emotions and frustrations ran rampant, from rebellion to resolve, from determination to fury. She tells her story eloquently, and readers will feel empathy without ever feeling pity. Since her case encompasses nearly every procedure used in scoliosis treatment, this book is a terrific resource for those who want to understand the condition and an excellent companion to the more academic "coping with-" titles. It also has clear black-and-white drawings, inspiring "after" photos, practical recommendations, and even a "word search" puzzle.
-Mary R. Hofmann, School Library Journal

# Testimonials

This young girl's informative narrative reveals her medical and emotional triumph over a potentially crippling condition. Michelle's story is deeply moving and candid. An absolute must for teens and their families. -Thomas and Madeleine Kohl Secondary and Elementary School Educators

Simple and sweetly told. The child conveys the struggle of growing up with scoliosis, but also the clarity and positive outlook that can come from staying strong. -Amazon Review

Scoliosis refers to the curving of the spine and is a medical condition that affects hundreds of teenage girls each year. Written and illustrated by Michelle Spray, Growing Up With Scoliosis: A Young Girl's Story addresses the emotional and social aspects arising from this condition and answers all the questions commonly raised by girls, friends, and family members affected by Scoliosis. Recommended by the National Scoliosis Foundation and a welcome addition to any medical clinic, community school or public library reference collection, Growing Up With Scoliosis is thoroughly "reader friendly" and simply invaluable in helping teens and families to cope with a condition that could otherwise have serious emotional ramifications. Midwest Book Review, 5-Star Amazon Review

This was a good book for my daughter. She is facing scoliosis surgery, and this was written by a girl who went through the same thing. Sometimes kids just need the opinion of another kid for the peace of mind. This book gave my daughter just that. She is not as fearful now and it answered many of her questions. Highly recommend if your child is facing scoliosis and the possibility of bracing or surgery. 5-Star Amazon Review

My eight year old daughter read it in two days ... could not stop. It was very informative and greatly told. I would recommend it. 5-Star Amazon Review

# Testimonials

This book Growing Up with Scoliosis is an inspirational, factual account by the author, on how she lived with and overcame her disability, during the most formative years of her life. One can only imagine the courage it took to relive her experiences, by committing them to paper, so that others would benefit. The images she creates makes the reader a silent partner in her initial discovery, extensive treatment and ultimate victory. Anyone who has scoliosis, or knows such a victim, indeed anyone with a long term illness will gain insight and hope from the experiences and emotions gleaned from the author's diary. The resulting book and the outcome are both sheer joy!
Stan Gorzelany

When I was 10 years old I was diagnosed with scoliosis. Like many young girls who have gone through this I thought that I had this horrible disease, that my life would never be the same. Unfortunately, I did not deal with this part of my life as bravely as Michelle Spray did. I experienced the Boston Brace. I was miserable and felt sorry for myself. My parents felt so bad for me that we didn't follow up with a doctor and I was allowed to throw the brace away after wearing it only for a year. Almost 20 years later I'm fortunate that my curvature did not get too horribly worse. I wish that I had had an account like Michelle's to help me understand that this was NOT the end of my world. Michelle's brave story of dealing with her scoliosis has inspired me. It should be required reading for all kids diagnosed. The story chronicles the 6 years of therapy and brace wearing for Michelle, with her curvature constantly progressing to the point where the risky spinal fusion operation was the best option. Michelle's positive attitude is incredibly refreshing. I cannot say enough how thrilled I am to have had a chance to read this. Way to go, Michelle!
Jeni, scoliosis patient and reader

# Testimonials

*Growing up with Scoliosis* by Michelle Spray, was such a pleasure to read. I really like this book. The story is interesting and well-written and makes for a nice, easy read for all ages. This book is great for parents or young Scoliosis patients alike. I read it in a few days and found that Michelle did an excellent job of taking a difficult time in her life, and putting a positive, lighthearted, and whimsical spin on it, through snippets and stories from her youth. Some of the information is out-of-date, as surgical procedures and recovery times and situations have changed dramatically, but the stories and emotions she experienced while growing up are still very applicable to patients today. -Tina at EmBraced in Comfort

Scoliosis refers to the curving of the spine and is a medical condition that affects hundreds of teenage girls each year. Written and illustrated by Michelle Spray, Growing Up With Scoliosis addresses the emotional and social aspects arising from this condition and answers all the questions commonly raised by girls, friends, and family members affected by Scoliosis. Recommended by the National Scoliosis Foundation and a welcome addition to any medical clinic, community school or public library reference collection, Growing Up With Scoliosis is thoroughly "reader friendly" and simply invaluable in helping teens and families to cope with a condition that could otherwise have serious emotional ramifications. The Midwest Book Review, Small Press Bookwatch, 8/03, Vol. 2, # 8

Growing Up With Scoliosis is the personal and heartfelt memoir of Michelle Spray, a young girl, who wrote down her thoughts as she adjusted to living with braces, posture exercises, and surgery to treat her scoliosis in the form of a spine curvature so severe it threatened to mercilessly twist her body. An upbeat and engaging true experience, highly recommended for young people everywhere who have to deal daily with this all-too-common condition, Growing Up With Scoliosis is especially recommended reading for young readers having to deal with scoliosis -- as well as their friends, families, neighbors, teachers, and providers. The Midwest Book Review- Small Press Bookwatch, 9/03, Vol. 2, # 9

# Dedication

This book is dedicated to my parents, Richard and Roberta Spray. They helped me through an emotional time in my life (and theirs), as I came to realize while writing this book. Thanks Mom and Dad for your patience, and understanding. Thank you to my siblings, who learned about "differences" very early in life.

# A Special Dedication

A special dedication to my grandmother Louise, who read this book in its early stages and loved the part about her the most. She would have enjoyed seeing this book become a reality.

# Acknowledgments

I would like to give a special thank-you to all the doctors, nurses, interns, and specialists I'd met during my journey with scoliosis. I especially want to thank Dr. Jerold Perlman for being gentle with my diagnosis, patient during the early stages, and for treating my scoliosis for as long as he could.

Thank you to Dr. Thomas Renshaw for treating my scoliosis in the more severe stages and particularly for his tremendous handiwork in my operation. My back is flat, my waistline is perfect, and my scar is hardly noticeable. (I was so worried about that!)

Special thanks also to Dr. Richard Diana and all the doctors, nurses, and specialists who worked together to make my surgery a success—before, during, and after the procedure.

# Additional thanks to

Tracy Weed, Mary Mahony, Susan Pasternack, and all my family and friends who have made this book possible.

# Special People

**Jerold Perlman, M.D.**, is a board-certified orthopaedic surgeon specializing in general orthopaedics and arthroscopic surgery in Fairfield, Connecticut. He received a B.A. from Columbia University and an M.D. from SUNY. In his spare time, Dr. Perlman enjoys golf, travel, and spending time with his family.

**Thomas Renshaw, M.D.**, is proudly enjoying retirement. While I was finishing this book, Dr. Renshaw was an orthopaedic surgeon and professor of orthopaedic surgery specializing in pediatric orthopaedics and spinal problems at Yale-New Haven Hospital in New Haven, Connecticut. He holds a B.S. and M.D. from Ohio State University. He has reviewed Growing Up with Scoliosis for its medical accuracy and graciously wrote the foreword.

**Connecticut Children's Medical Center** (formerly Newington Children's Hospital) is a wonderful pediatric, teaching and research hospital for children from birth to age 18. They are "dedicated to the physical and emotional health of your child..." Their motto is: "Kids are great, we just make 'em better." http:// www.ccmckids.org.

**Susan Pasternack** is an editor and writer in Newton, Massachusetts. She edits a variety of works, but admits that scoliosis has become a topic of special interest. She has also edited two scoliosis books by Mary Mahony, There's an 'S' on my Back and What Can I Give You. In her free time, she enjoys reading, traveling, and spending time with her family.

**Tracy Weed** is the owner of TWeed Photography, is a West Hartford, CT photographer and jewelry designer. In her spare time, she is either on stage or working on her first novel. You can view her portrait work at: http://www.tweedphotography.photobiz. com and shop The Tiny Wren, her line of handmade, vintage style jewelry at: https://www.etsy.com/shop/thetinywren

These special people made this book possible.

# Helpful Links

Helpful Links: http://www.allaboutscoliosis.com/helpful-links

SpineUniverse.com contains a wealth of knowledge for Scoliosis patients of all ages and stages: https://www.spineuniverse.com/conditions/scoliosis

The Global Scoliosis Foundation explains the different Types Of Scoliosis: http://www.globalscoliosis.com/types-of-scoliosis

Scoliosis Research Society shares Patient Stories: http://www.srs.org/patient_and_family/patient_stories

Scoliosis Family Adventures: Supports families of scoliosis patients with a wonderful blog: http://scoliosisfamilyadventures.wordpress.com/2014/02/15/update-on-embraced-in-comfort

EmBraced In Comfort: is a Made in the USA company that designs and manufactures undergarments for use with Scoliosis braces: www.embracedincomfort.com

Scoliosis Correction, treatments, & options: http://www.morenojosephspine.com/procedures/scoliosis-correction

SHIFT Scoliosis: Shifting the way the world sees Scoliosis: www.shiftscoliosis.org/#!samis-story/cjg9

Scoliosis: What You Need to Know: http://www.spine-health.com/conditions/scoliosis/scoliosis-what-you-need-know

The National Scoliosis Foundation (NSF) is a patient-led nonprofit scoliosis organization since 1976 http://www.scoliosis.org/nsf.php

Options to help you get back to doing the things you love: http://www.back.com/back-pain/conditions/scoliosis/

# Word Search

```
I L O C S H T I W P U G N I W O
S N V E I D I O P A T H I C B R
D C E L A T E R A L U M B A R G
N R U E A X R Y T R E B U P K Y
E E V I T I S O P W U L L F C A
I D I A G N O S I S W O L O R R
R O T C O D R E D C R O S S X P
F C U T S I D E A P O H T R O S
H A P P Y C U R V E K C A B N E
P U W O L L O F O S I S H E U L
S O D S B M U L X R A Y C S R L
C T E I S T R A I G H T T I S E
O C G L A T R A R O I P E C E H
L O R S C O L E I P S D R R E C
I D E O P A N F R I E I T E C I
C H E C K I O R C L E V S X A M
N R S O P P M E E T S E H E R X
X E T S E C N E I R E P X E B Y
```

| | | |
|---|---|---|
| back | experiences | puberty |
| brace | follow up | red cross |
| check | friends | school |
| curve | happy | scoliosis |
| degrees | idiopathic | spine |
| diagnosis | lateral | straight |
| dive | lumbar | stretch |
| doctor | nurse | teen |
| esteem | orthopaedist | velcro |
| exercise | positive | xray |

# Word Scramble

kacb      _____

craeb      _____

rucve      _____

iooslciss      _____

igoidanss      _____

roctod      _____

eeemts      _____

sixrecee      _____

I want you to know you're my inspiration too! I'd love to hear from you. michellespraybooks@gmail.com
Good luck on your journey!

82963974R00070

Made in the USA
Lexington, KY
08 March 2018